House of Correction

Also by Simon Hoggart and published by Robson Books

On the House
Back on the House
House of Ill Fame

House of Correction

Simon Hoggart

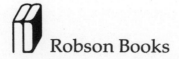 Robson Books

First published in Great Britain in 1994
by Robson Books Ltd, Bolsover House,
5–6 Clipstone Street, London W1P 7EB

**British Library Cataloguing in Publica-
tion Data**
A catalogue record for this title is
available from the British Library

ISBN 0 86051 943 0

Photoset in North Wales by Derek Doyle &
Associates, Mold, Clwyd. Printed in Great Britain
by Butler & Tanner Ltd, Frome and London.

Introduction

On a recent visit to the United States I found that our House of Commons had become cult viewing on cable television. The term 'cult' usually implies that, although the word of mouth is good, no one is actually watching. That may well be the case. However, I do get questions from American friends: 'What's this "right honourable" shit they're laying down?' was one. Jack Wetherill, the previous Speaker, says that he is still recognized in the streets of American cities, even without his wig. One magazine heralded the arrival of our legislators on their screens with the advice: 'Check these guys out. They're *animals!*'

Well, not really, though television cameras do strange things to people. TV in the Commons has had some definite effects. In Prime Minister's Questions, it has led to short discussions being replaced by even shorter sound-bites. It's a myth that there was a time when Prime Minister's Questions took the form of a Socratic dialogue, though it was Harold Wilson who decided – long before the cameras – that it should become a joust between prime minister and Opposition leader. Wilson realized that he could generally get the better of Sir Alec Douglas-Home, and that his successes would trickle down to back benchers, party workers and the electorate.

But there was, I think, still some extempore speaking. These days both sides arrive with questions and answers written out beforehand, and plough through them irrespective of what the fellow across the Despatch Box says. The effect is to create a bizarre series of *non sequiturs*, along these lines:

> *Opposition leader:* Will the prime minister condemn the absolutely disgraceful fact, X?
> *Prime minister:* I notice that you have not taken this opportunity to condemn the equally disgraceful fact, Y!
> *Opposition leader:* So, the prime minister will not answer my question! Will he or will he not tell the British people whether he condemns X?
> *Prime minister:* I'm a little teapot, short and stout! Tip me up and pour me out!
> *Opposition leader:* The whole nation will notice that the prime minister has feigned lunacy in order to avoid answering my question ...

In the real world, the prime minister has behind him a host of sycophants only too eager to ask questions planted by the whips and designed to allow him to recite whatever lovingly chamfered statistic is in his head. At one point I thought of giving a *Guardian* Greasy Spoon award to the most creepy question of the week, but it would have been too predictable. What is distressing is that this kind of obsequious behaviour does seem to work. In my experience, powerful men generally despise those who suck up to them. Mr Major, by contrast, gives them preferment.

Working through my reports from the Press Gallery for this book, I discovered that two of the greasiest MPs had obtained ministerial jobs in the summer reshuffle, and there may well be others whose oleaginous contributions I missed. It seems perverse of the prime minister to demand a reform of Question Time while repaying the very people who help to make it an expense of spirit and a waste of shame.

Yet this is at the heart of the problem. There are complaints these days that power has deserted the House of Commons and is now vested mainly with the government (as well as with the European Union, the civil service, the judiciary and the innumerable unelected quangos). This is a genuine vicious circle. Since back benchers can only obtain real influence by becoming ministers, they have no interest in acting as a check on the ministers who are already in office. The more power the executive seizes, the more it is given, because succumbing to the executive's will is the only way to join it. In theory, there is no reason why the whips shouldn't scour the corridors for the independent minded, for free spirits guided only by their judgement and their consciences. Fat chance. Winston Smith tried to hate Big Brother at least for a while.

Meanwhile, I suspect that the real debate has switched to television. There has never been so much politics on TV. While the main evening news programmes demand the quick 15-second quote, daytime news shows include lengthy political debates. So does Channel 4 News. There's a political programme on Channel 4 every lunchtime now. The *People's Parliament* began in the summer of 1994, as if to demonstrate that ordinary members of the public could do better than their elected representatives. Throw in *Newsnight*, Brian Walden's weekly interview, *On the Record*, *The Week in Politics*, *Breakfast with Frost*, BBC's *Breakfast Time* (Channel 4's *Big Breakfast* admittedly features politicians rather less often than members of 'Wet Wet Wet') plus innumerable special reports, daytime discussions, regional programming and talk shows – the line between politicians and any other chattering celebrity is increasingly blurred – and I suspect there is as much discussion of political issues on TV as there is on the floor of the Commons, much of it more informative and comprehensible.

My favourite description of the House is old, but worth repeating. An elderly Labour MP, a retired miner called Bill Stone, was sitting in the corner of the Strangers' Bar drowning the pain in his lungs with Federation bitter. At the bar itself a group of journalists and MPs were discussing the quality of the present intake. One of them, exasperated, declared: 'The trouble with this place is that it's full of cunts!'

Stone put down his pint, wiped his mouth, and remarked: 'There's plenty of cunts in t'country, and they deserve some representation.'

It's a good definition of what any legislature ought to be like. But are there more cunts now than before? It's a question which one asks now and again, and usually provides oneself with the answer 'yes'. This may have to do with growing older. For what it's worth, I suspect that the quality of a party's intake is counter-cyclical with its hold on a majority. Labour's recent recruits are the best for a long time, and will be needed if the party is ever to return to power. (The shortage of good newcomers in the late 1970s was exposed by the death of John Smith: to stand a chance of being taken seriously the party had to go straight to someone elected in 1983.)

The Tories seem to me to be doing worse during the eighties, with Julian Critchley's *Garagistes* being joined by stars of daytime television and other undesirables. You can trace the decline through the people they elect to the 1922 Executive where serious people such as Geoffrey Johnson Smith have been joined by drolls such as David Evans (whose attempts to turn his wife Janice into a well-loved national archetype have died like some fifth-rate comedian on an end-of-pier talent show).

Here are some of the questions I tend to be asked by people who marvel that anyone could bear to sit in the Commons Press Gallery for a living.

– Do MPs hate what you write about them?

Yes, some do, but the great majority regard criticism of themselves as a small price to pay for reading rude things about their colleagues. As my old boss Ian Aitken of the *Guardian* told me when I started as a political reporter: 'Whenever you make one enemy in Parliament, you automatically make 650 friends.'

Oddly enough, wives often enjoy seeing their husbands traduced. Twice I have been sought out at social events by women who wanted to thank me for some particularly offensive remark about their spouse.

– Why do they shout at each other all the time?

Well, they don't really, except during Prime Minister's Questions, which amounts to only half an hour a week. Much of the time the Chamber is largely deserted. I do not find this particularly shocking; MPs must now act as social workers for much of their day, and this means they have more important things to do than listen to other MPs speaking.

If they do have something to say, they would rather say it on TV. It is literally the case that there can be more Members of Parliament on College Green – the patch of grass which you always see on television because it offers a good view of Big Ben in the background – than there are in the Chamber.

– What *is* all this 'right honourable' shit?

The term 'honourable member' – while obviously a ludicrous epithet for many MPs – is supposed to encourage courtesy in the Chamber by slowing down the tongue and forcing MPs to articulate a phrase which they generally don't mean. 'Right honourable' refers to a member of Her Majesty's Privy Council, a title which comes with the job of cabinet minister, plus a few others. It doesn't imply that the holder is any more honest, upright or unlikely to bandy about a lady's name in public than anyone else.

– Why does the prime minister always say: 'I refer the

honourable member to the answer I gave some moments ago'? What's he talking about?

Years ago, prime ministers used to evade questions by passing them on to the minister in charge of whichever department they might conceivably relate. So MPs got round that by asking him, or her, whether he had plans to visit Eatanswill – or whatever the name of their constituency was. He would reply that he had no immediate plans to do so. The MP would then get in his supplementary: 'When he does, will he take the opportunity to remind the electors of Eatanswill of the government's remarkable achievements/catastrophic failures ...'

That device fell out of fashion, and now he is merely asked what his engagements for the day are. These invariably turn out to be 'meetings with ministerial colleagues and others'. The formula gives the prime minister a few extra moments to ponder his reply and allows the MP to ask whatever supplementary he had planned anyway. It all contributes to the weird, other-worldly air which clings to the Commons, and increasingly makes the voters sense that its deliberations have little to do with them or their problems.

And yet, even now the House can – very occasionally – grasp a topic and shake it, crystallize a national mood, or illuminate a point which might have otherwise escaped the light. Like Mr Kenneth Clarke, who will attend a reserve team football fixture in the rain if there is nothing else on, we fans treasure these rare moments and are prepared to sit through much boredom to find them.

Every year it is the Liberal Democrats who hold the first party conference of the season.

Little changes at the Liberal conference except, periodically, the name of the party. They assembled at Torquay, all those half-remembered bald men with beards and ecologically sound shoes, the gentle herbivorous women offering passers-by leaflets on site value rating, and those magnificent Liberal motions, describing in anally retentive detail how to save the British economy, or rural bus services, all partitioned into separate watertight segments, like the *Titanic*.

Were it not for the presence of Lord Jenkins with his faint whiff of Romeo y Julieta cigars and Château Latour, his air of knowing about a distant, cosmopolitan world outside, one would feel that this was the political equivalent of a train spotters' convention.

The most controversial debate of the day was on ethnic minorities, a source of some embarrassment to the party since the allegations were made of racism down among the Liberals who run Tower Hamlets. Finding racism anywhere in the LibDems clearly came as a gruesome surprise, the equivalent of finding an anaconda in your anorak.

So of course the debate wasn't actually controversial at all. The only argument was about who could be even less racist than the rest. They arrived at the podium quivering with anti-racism. They are so anti-racist that as the main speaker, Ramesh Dewan, pointed out, white people were welcome – even encouraged – to join the party's ethnic

1

minorities group. This was fortunate, since a glance round the hall made it clear this would otherwise be a very small band indeed.

The best speech of the day came from Charles Kennedy, who, like Lord Jenkins, used to be a member of the SDP, a party you may vaguely remember. Near him was a young woman who was signing for the deaf. But of course Roy was signing too, with a selection of his own best-loved hand gestures.

Mr Kennedy attacked the Labour Party and Lord Jenkins started to strangle someone. Mr Kennedy moved on to Norman Lamont and Lord Jenkins began washing his hands. John Major was scorned, and Lord Jenkins prepared to play the piano. Mr Kennedy spoke about the rot in British politics, and Lord Jenkins began chopping wood.

The real signer got tired and paused (I could see no evidence of any deaf people in the audience, but that's not the point. When you are terrifically worthy but have no prospect of power, even your gestures have to be gestures.) All my attention was focused on Lord Jenkins. How one yearned to see the famous cupped, scooping motion with which he enlivened so many of his fine speeches at the time of the Gang of Four.

All it needed was for Mr Kennedy to announce: 'Fellow Liberals, we must replace burnt out light bulbs!' Or even, 'We must caress the bosoms of young women!'

21 September 1993

Liberals always have the best names. My favourite regular delegate at their conferences is one Hester Smallbone, though I have not seen her this year. No doubt she has returned to whichever Thomas Hardy novel from which she was on leave.

The debate on constitutional reform was opened by the magnificently monickered Mr Andrew Adonis. Unfortunately, though you couldn't actually call him ugly, Mr Adonis did have an unnerving resemblance to Sir Norman Fowler.

One toyed with the idea that it might actually be Sir Norman. He'd certainly be safer here in Torquay among these ruminative folk than he would with the hunter-killers at the Tory conference next month.

Anyhow, Sir Norman was introducing a magnificent baroque version of a Liberal resolution, a Salzburg Cathedral among motions, bedecked with ornately carved sections, clauses, sub-clauses, codicils and curlicues. These lads do not care for the broad brush, the statement of intent slapped on like Snowcem. And if you wanted even more details, there was a policy document on the subject which contained one entire ready-made, off-the-peg constitution for the whole United Kingdom, including no fewer than 292 sub-sections.

This document had it all. I could not find anything they'd missed. They even included, literally, the abolition of slavery, debtors' prisons, arranged marriages and the Salic Law on royal succession. ('Gender' is to be ignored altogether when it comes to getting a new sovereign. Presumably sexist words such as 'king' and 'queen' will be abolished too, and like Liberal chairpersons, the monarch will simply be addressed as 'Throne'.)

The delegates proudly examined their new constitution, like Billy Liar reviewing his imaginary army. It's a phenomenon often noted at Liberal conferences: they mysteriously believe that because they have voted on something, it has actually happened. 'We haven't abolished the monarchy, but we have abolished the royal prerogative,' raved one young man as if, well, as if they had abolished it.

Later they debated the energy tax. I felt sorry for them.

Quite unexpectedly, the decision to put VAT on domestic fuel has infuriated many Tory voters and has helped to win two by-elections so far for the LibDems. Yet the party is committed to putting its own thumping great tax on energy too.

Now, you will understand that there is a world of difference between these two taxes. Whereas Mr Lamont's was a grubby and cynical attempt to raise funds for a morally bankrupt government, the Liberal tax is part of a high-minded crusade to save the planet. Sadly, both taxes would have to be paid with money, and the voters may not perceive this crucial difference.

22 September 1993

When Paddy Ashdown went to see Patsy Rodenburg, who is 'Head of Voice' at the National Theatre, she told him that since the cameras in the House of Commons look down, he should look up. This works well on TV, but is one reason why the dislike of Paddy (or 'Jeremy', his real name) in the House goes beyond the normal discourtesies. MPs suspect he is not really talking to them, and they're right. He is the first post-TV party leader.

In his closing speech to the Liberal Democrat conference, he spent much of his time gazing upwards as if at a vision. It was disconcerting. He looked like a painting of the Annunciation, with Mr Vivien White of the BBC in place of the Angel Gabriel.

He has some oddly old-fashioned face language (which is like body language, only tougher and more determined). When he is moved by his own words, which happens often, he juts out his jaw and stretches his face around it, making him the only British military hero with a stiff lower lip.

The speech contained some good gags, one at the expense of Sir Arthur Comyns-Carr, who was the Liberal foreign affairs spokesman 40 years ago. He had once begun an address: 'I do not wish to say anything which might endanger the security of Quemoy and Matsu ...' The joke, with its implication that nowadays the Chinese government does care what's said at a Liberal conference, went down well. Other parties like to recall their glorious past; it's a measure of Ashdown's self-confidence that he sees the pre-Ashdownian past as the wilderness years, ended by his own guidance.

Indeed the past, apart from one mention of Lord Halifax, scarcely got a look in. His references are nearly all to TV: *Spitting Image*, or the Prudential commercial. Our statesmen used to quote Shakespeare and Milton to us; soon our common ground will be only Noel Edmunds and the Gold Blend couple.

Mr Ashdown's main fault as a speaker is that he not only offers us clichés; he seems to relish them. 'Let me warn you ... tough decisions lie ahead ... our greatest single asset will be the skills and ideas of our people!'

He did invent a new truism. 'We're going to have to find a new language which expresses taxation not as a burden, but as an opportunity!' he declared.

This translates as 'so people will vote for us even though we want to tax them more'. It will be a remarkable trick if he can pull it off.

A Liberal asked me what I thought of the speech. I said judiciously that it had been around ten times better than John Major's would be at the Tory conference.

'Huh,' he snorted, 'typical journalist, you can't ever find a good word to say about us Liberals.'

24 September 1993

The Labour conference was held in Brighton. It turned out to be John Smith's second, and last, as leader. He gained a difficult victory. However, the press had marked him down as boring and ineffectual, a charge held against him until the day he died, when everyone – in the space of half an hour – realized he had been neither. The big news on the first day was that Tony Benn lost his seat on the party's national executive, after 34 years.

The room was packed, waiting for what everyone really knew already. It had been predicted for months, but the shock – the sense that an era in British politics might be ending for ever – was none the less for that. There was a gasp when it happened, followed by an almost audible sense of relief. Thank goodness that's over, the party seemed to be saying, now we can move on.

Yes, Hattie Hayridge, a comedienne at the 'Women Only' revue on the eve of the conference, told a heterosexist joke, depending for its humorous impact on the notion that a woman might actually want to have sexual relations with a man, indicating a great seismic shift, a grinding of Labour's tectonic plates. She complained that Tampax had crammed instructions on the box in so many languages that all they had room for was 'Insert into vagina'. 'I suppose if you were on holiday and in bed with a Greek waiter, you could point to it,' she said. The audience roared with laughter.

Marjorie Mowlam, the front bencher who had organized the evening, beamed with relief. 'That could never have happened ten years ago,' she said. 'The party really has changed.'

Oh, and Mr Benn lost his seat on the NEC. Sadly, I have to report that this caused glee among other Labour MPs.

I have often wondered why this courteous, faintly dotty old gentleman arouses such hatred among his colleagues, and have concluded that it is his amiable public nature that probably riles them most – it's like being given a moral lecture by M. Hulot while he steals your travellers' cheques.

Mr Benn took his defeat with good humour and grace, waving to the applause. An MP near me said that he wanted to spit.

You can see how much the conference has changed. MPs are allowed to speak without being booed. There are even attacks on the Conservatives, which not long ago would have been thought an irrelevant frivolity by many of the comrades.

There were occasional reminders of the past. I heard the word 'socialism' twice. A woman in the health debate declared: 'Reality is not working!' a slogan which has served the hard left well for many years.

But the success of the new regime was clear from the start, with the vote on smoking in the hall. This was ruthlessly determined on the principles of One Member, One Vote (OMOV), with no block vote. The chairman decreed: 'I don't think we'll bother with those against.' Mr Smith must have thought he had died and gone to party leaders' paradise.

28 September 1993

For some weird reason, the Labour Party has always had its leader's speech on the Tuesday morning of the annual conference. This means that the remaining three days of the session are a long anti-climax, though so immense is the power of conservatism in the party that nobody has ever thought to alter this arrangement.

The Labour Party doesn't yet love John Smith, though perhaps one day it will. His speech yesterday was vigorous, combative, high-minded and just a little flat. They like him and respect him; yesterday they were relieved by his performance. But he hasn't yet engaged them.

Of course it wasn't his fault that yesterday's speeches included two, by John Prescott and Dennis Skinner, which won spontaneous standing ovations and disproved the belief that the deadening acoustics of the Brighton Conference Centre turn all speeches into instant rabble-soothers.

Mr Prescott's speech was fine, roaring polemic. The delegates adored it, and none more than Mr Prescott himself, who at the end sat applauding himself, with evident sincerity.

Dennis Skinner's speech was a cunning pastiche of a Dennis Skinner speech. He spoke about the marches against the pit closures. 'Those were glorious days,' he said, twice. The delegates, who had given him a humiliating vote in the national executive elections, cheered him dementedly.

Before he took up politics, Mr Skinner used to tour the pubs and clubs of his native Clay Cross, wearing a drape jacket and singing Elvis Presley songs. Possibly he also believes that reports of Elvis's death were got up by the Tory press.

So Mr Smith had a difficult job from the start. In this respect the Labour Party resembles the Prince of Wales. It had been under pressure to do the right thing and choose a sensible practical sort of person. Having done so, it loyally carried out its duties with that person, even managing to smile in the right places. But it still can't wait to get home and talk to Mrs Parker Bowles.

Faced with the fact that all attacks on the Conservatives have been made innumerable times over the past 14 years, Mr Smith, like a junkie with a punctured arm, managed to find new places to insert the needle. It was a highly moral speech, a sermon on the nature of human wickedness. Mr Smith sees recent administrations not just as dogmatic incompetents, but as deeply corrupt, deploying their policies only to permit power and wealth to pursue each other. It's a world in which normal human decency is ignored or even despised, where money is the only measure of worth, and its distribution decided by those who already have too much of it.

It was a dark and depressing vision, a voyage to the outer suburbs of the Inferno. What it lacked was a map for getting us out. 'Repent, repent!' is a tried and tested slogan, but it doesn't amount to a manifesto.

29 September 1993

John Smith won his critical vote on One Member, One Vote, by a hair's breadth, thanks in part to a rumbustious speech by Mr John Prescott.

'It's carrying democracy too far if you don't know the result before the vote,' the late Bert Wynn of the National Union of Mineworkers used to say. Yesterday Mr Smith carried democracy as far as it would stretch. Was his victory a dazzling strategic success, or a cock-up which somehow came right? As usual, it was both.

At the end Mr Smith smiled the biggest smile I've ever seen on him. It wasn't his anxious smile, or the cheeky chappie smile which means that he's thought of a new joke against a colleague, but the big broad smile of the man who knows he is in charge. The weight seemed to fall back on him. Give him a silk hat and he would have been the Fat Controller.

Yesterday was a magical return to the days when Labour conferences were unpredictable and fun. All day long knots of seedy men smoking cheap cigarettes stood in huddles, whispering from the corners of their mouths, scribbling numbers on the back of beer mats. But then the press always over-reacts. The union leaders seemed more jocular and relaxed, almost statesmanlike by comparison.

The party ended with, it is being said, a new de facto deputy leader after John Prescott's bravura performance to close the debate. Up to a point. The deputy leader's job is rather dull, mostly involving attendance at dreary meetings. What Mr Prescott has become is Official Conference Darling, a far more agreeable role.

It's an extraordinary act. The OCD started off at little more than normal volume, when he described his own working life – 'ten years of seafaring' – when he worked as a bar steward. Then it was yo-ho-ho and a Harvey Wall-banger, the wind filled his sails, and we were off on the tide. The voice rose, the hands began to swing like yard-arms, the syntax fell overboard. Entirely inappropriate words began to appear in unexpected places, as if the OCD had hurled the speech into the air and re-assembled it at random. Sometimes he seemed to be advocating the opposite of his case, but with undiminished passion.

No matter. The delegates adored him. The OCD had offered them what every delegate wants, which is validation. Permission to vote the way they felt they ought to. It may have turned the conference.

Later Joyce Gould, the former Labour official, told the

BBC: 'John talks to the delegates in a language they can understand.' This is nonsense; nobody can understand his language. What Mrs Gould meant was that he has the most useful gift any politician can have: it doesn't matter what he says, because everyone knows what he means.

The day began with a sense of relief. At last all this soppy Tory bashing could end, and they could get on with their traditional job of bashing each other. Mr Smith's speech was better than yesterday's because it was more sharply focused and because the concessions they were waiting for did not come. The boot never dropped.

'I ask the party to trust its members,' he said, which would be a startling innovation in a party which no more trusts its members than it trusts that even more treacherous body, the electorate.

Jimmy Knapp of RMT, the transport union, was bold and passionate. At least I assume he was, since I couldn't comprehend a word he said and spent the time marvelling that this vast, stooped, bald man, who looks like a polar bear attacked by a lawn strimmer, is almost precisely the same age as Cliff Richard.

Bill Morris was awful. As he finished, the only real applause came from the T and G delegates who stood together, alone for him, giving us a last sighting of the block vote, an ancient British tradition now destined to go the same way as Maypole dancing and Simon Bates.

30 September 1993

I bumped into Norman Tebbit at the Labour conference yesterday. He was doing TV work but, even so, I thought he was being foolhardy, like Gordon at Khartoum, or Michael Howard at a policemen's ball.

He said it was all right, since the delegates assumed he was a holographic image. 'Actually, we often have friendly conversations,' he said. 'I find them very pleasant and polite, but then most people are.' Then he nutted me.

I made that last bit up. But it says a lot about declining standards in our public life that a right-wing former Tory minister can walk about a Labour conference unharmed. Not long ago Lord Tebbit would have been reduced to his constituent parts, leaving only a pair of wire glasses and a wax doll of Tristan Garel-Jones, but young people today seem to have no disrespect for their elders. I blame the courts. Send 'em on a few more Club Med holidays; that'll teach them.

But the whole conference is eerily placid. In the defence debate they passed a motion which almost said that we should make more weapons in order to keep defence workers in jobs. This could have led to some grand flights of oratory. 'Comrades, are we mad? With the money we are now wasting on new schools, we could build a desperately needed nuclear submarine! Instead of pouring money into the bottomless pit of the NHS, we could have more wire-guided missiles!'

But even David Coates, who moved the resolution against Trident, matched the soporific mood. Mr Coates is from the furniture union, and he was called by the chair to speak on the motion he had tabled. He was, frankly, wooden. His speech lacked polish. It fell between two stools. It was couched in boring terms. What we needed was the Member for Chesterfield.

Suddenly, there was Mr Benn, and the conference flickered briefly to life. It was a short, glorious reminder of old-fashioned Bennery: his 'minor contribution' to four election victories on a socialist platform (Benn is one of the few people who uses understatement as a form of hyperbole), the generation of hope that built the welfare state, and so forth. He won a standing ovation from the delegates who had voted him off the national executive only three days before.

More and more this conference is coming to resemble a sharp-suited nephew who offers sympathy and comfort at the Twilight Retirement Home while cleaning out his aunt's deposit account.

1 October 1993

The Tory conference was heralded by two other events. Lady Thatcher's memoirs were leaked to the *Daily Mirror*, and we learned about the many affairs enjoyed by Mr Steven Norris.

Lady Thatcher arrived in Blackpool like a character from Oscar Wilde. Not Lady Bracknell – far too mild mannered – but Gwendoline, who also wrote memoirs in order to have something sensational to read on the train.

Yesterday the hunt was on for the source of the leaks which revealed her contempt for John Major. Clearly it must be someone with intimate knowledge of the memoirs, someone who covertly despises Major and wanted this to be known.

One imagines the phone ringing in the *Daily Mirror* office. A curiously muffled voice comes on the line. 'Now, pin back yer lugholes and cop this, me old china, me old mate!'

'Ah, good morning Lady Thatcher.'

Mr Major is coming to resemble another well-loved British character who has taken enough punishment and ought to consider retirement. Like Frank Bruno, he could go into pantomime. One could catch him in, say, Harrogate, along with other half-remembered figures such as Billy Dainty, Helen Shapiro and 'John Major as Buttons'.

But the saddest figure on the platform yesterday was Steven Norris, the transport minister. The *Sun* had pictures of no fewer than four of his mistresses on its front page yesterday. His head must whirl with double meanings – underpasses and box junctions, contraflows and gyratory systems. Mr Norris looked steeped in misery throughout. One longed for him to hear from a cheerful cockney clippie: 'Never mind dear, room for one more on top.'

6 October 1993

Her ladyship skulked in her room for the second day.

The most terrifying platform performer at the Tory conference yesterday was a Mr Andrew Boff, who lives in Brick Lane in the East End of London. Mr Boff is a big man, with stubble on his head rather than hair, protruding brows, bulging eyeballs, and when cross, which seems to be often, a magnificent spittle-flecked snarl. He looked like a rottweiler in a Paul Smith suit.

The delegates, who love anyone who looks different from them but cranks out the identical nonsense, cheered him wildly in the environment debate, even when he came out with the most improbable line of the conference so far: 'I am fighting for the Conservatives because of subsidiarity!'

Later, the Home Secretary's speech described how some of our most ancient rights are to be removed as a consequence of the government's failures. It was either a promise of invigorating action, or a shameless, populist rant. I can't tell you which, because I was transfixed by his extraordinary speaking voice. Mr Howard's problem is vowel sounds. When in doubt, he chooses the letter 'I'. 'Pipple want to slip siffley in their homes ... gitting tiff on criminils in pissfull villages or liffy suburbs ... supporting the pilliss ...'

It was hypnotic, and of course rapturously received. Crime debates are the Tory equivalent of a John Prescott speech: they have only a glancing connection with the real world, only delegates can understand them, but they recall a happier era.

7 October 1993

Finally, she appeared on the platform.

The Tory conference rose to acclaim its lost leader. There must have been hundreds in the hall who wondered ruefully just what they had thrown away three careless years before.

It was pungently nostalgic. The shimmering clothes, the beautifully coiffed blonde hair, the gracious smile with the familiar steely glint still lurking in those hard blue eyes. They cheered, whooped and whistled, till it seemed that the whole conference would grind to a rapturous halt.

Indeed, Michael Heseltine's first public appearance since his heart attack was greeted with something near dementia. His reception was notably better than the one for Lady Thatcher. It must have been terribly galling for her.

She arrived at around 10.30. The car sped straight into the building. One half expected it to drive onstage. Dame Wendy Mitchell, the conference chairman (no Liberal gender confusion here) announced coyly: 'Hold on, ladies and gentlemen, I think we are going to have a visitor!'

Lady Thatcher appeared on stage and sat next to Basil Feldman, chairwoman of the Tories' National Union. There was applause, all right, lots of it, but very many people remained seated and much of the clapping was artificially prolonged by her claque of irreconcilables.

This annual arrival is now a fixed event in Britain's calendar of colourful rituals and is conducted according to various time-honoured rules. At one point Lady Thatcher leans over to the chairperson and indicates that she would like to hear the debate. Everyone knows this is the signal for the clapping to redouble, though yesterday it actually began to fade. Must we lose all our old traditions?

Many of the delegates are rather angry with her about the leaked criticisms of John Major. For herself, she is clearly suffering from PMT or Pre-Memoir Tension. The curse is come upon her, like the Lady of Shalott, who also had trouble with the Mirror.

Cunningly, John Major arrived on the platform half an hour later. A brief handshake (to kiss or not to kiss? Always a tricky social teaser, except when you loathe each other). He won far and away the loudest stander of the day.

Later Ken Clarke made a gentle sort of speech, quietly received. There were two theories about this. Either, with his threat of higher taxes, he was trying to treat the delegates like grown-ups – always a high-risk strategy at the Tory conference. Or else it was a double-bluff. A tub-thumping rant would have appeared disloyal, so harming his leadership chances. In order to appear a better man than John Major, he had to make a worse speech. Imagine if your job depended on such calculations, every single day.

8 October 1993

Sensibly, the Tory leader's speech winds up the
conference on the Friday afternoon, so providing a
climax of sorts. Unknown to us at the time, the speech
contained one particular hostage to fortune ...

John Major's speech yesterday wasn't great – it never is –
but it was rousingly adequate, even thrillingly average.
The jokes were almost funny, the tone nearly assured, the
peroration on the brink of being moving.

Afterwards a colleague said to me: 'It's not every day
you learn the solution to one of life's great mysteries –
how do horses sleep standing up?' But he was better than
that. At the risk of damning with faint praise, it may have
been the best speech he's ever made.

Of course, the delegates were desperate to applaud.
They would have cheered him crazily if he had read out a
speech by John Prescott. The Conservatives have now
elected Mr Prescott as their new Socialist Bogeyman,
replacing Tony Benn who, you may be sure, will soon
re-emerge as a symbol of the old-fashioned decency now
jettisoned by the Labour Party. In fact, just before the
prime minister began, they ran a jokey video of Mr
Prescott's celebrated conference speech last week –
backwards. And yes, you still knew exactly what he was
talking about.

Major has the opposite problem. The speech is
coherent and grammatical, the individual words all make
sense, but at the end you're still not clear just what he
meant.

The greatest cheers were for the greatest truisms. Lady
Thatcher says that he is over-impressed by platitudes. He
certainly likes them. He even finds them inspiring. He
speaks them with the awed certainty of someone who has
just learned the secret of life from a Tibetan monk with
three eyes.

'Crime cannot be excused, and I give you my word' –

the voice drops confidentially – 'that under my government, it never will be!' What can that mean? Did anyone imagine that the Tories were going to send ramraiders on Club 18-30 holidays? As platitudes go, that was duck-billed.

His problem is this: how can the country be in such a mess when our lot have been running it for the past 14 years? He coped in two ways. First he blamed the fashionable orthodoxies of the 1960s which had destroyed schools, family life and respect for law and order. It was time, he said, to get 'back to basics'.

Abbie Hoffman, or some other bearded American, once said that if you could remember the sixties, you couldn't have been there. That, for John Major, is their great attraction. He wasn't there, so he can't be blamed.

Secondly, he implies that after 14 years of Tory misrule, it's time for a change. He talks about, for example, crime as if he had inherited the whole boiling from the last bunch of incompetents who were in office – which, of course, is exactly what he did. The Tories, he implied, were now going to clean up the mess left them by the Conservative Party. After the speech, some MPs were even thinking the unthinkable: that he might still be leader at the same time next year.

So, as the delegates trooped off home, they were at least united in their unstinting praise for the man whose performance has dominated the headlines all week, the transport minister Steven Norris. As one of his colleagues said, 'To have one mistress is a peccadillo. To have two is a scandal. But to have five is a matter for the most profound admiration.'

9 October 1993

Almost every year, between the party conferences in October and the State Opening in early November, there is a spill-over period in which loose odds and ends of business are concluded.

It turns out that there is a gaping hole in Britain's defences. It is, the defence secretary Malcolm Rifkind told the Commons, the name of the new, second-level medal for people who are not sufficiently gallant to win the Victoria Cross for valour, but are nevertheless a jolly sight more valiant than people on the third level of bravery.

This will be the new classless society version of the Distinguished Service Order, open to all ranks. The DSO will continue to be awarded for 'command and leadership' – which means in practice that only officers will win it, but never mind. It is the egalitarian thought which counts.

There will be another medal for anyone, field marshal or squaddie, who is approximately as gallant as the typical averagely gallant DSO. It is this which so far lacks a name.

I would suggest calling it the Military Award for Leadership (Commanders Or Lower ranks) Medal, or MALCOLM for short. It would be a fitting tribute to the first truly Thatcherite defence secretary.

For in spite of her rudeness about him ('unpredictable ... erratic ... childish') this was a defence speech which would have delighted any free marketeer. In the past our heroes were military men, famed for their courage in the face of the enemy. Now we celebrate cost-cutters and market-share enhancers.

For instance, the new slimmed-down Territorial Army will be employed increasingly in real operations, marking perhaps the first time that the regular army has resorted to using temps.

The royal dockyards are to be privatized, Mr Rifkind

said, 'to conduct their business in a commercial environment' and to 'diversify into other markets', such as, perhaps, video rental and photocopying.

Even the new fourth-level medal, for people whose gallantry is barely distinguishable from whimpering cowards like you and me, is to be called the Queen's Commendation for Valuable Services, which sounds like the military equivalent of the watch and jokey willie-warmer people get after working 35 years in the accounts department.

It all sounded a little like Birt of the BBC. Soon we can expect 'Officer Choice', so that when a brigadier requires air cover, he phones round a few combat squadrons for estimates. By that time they'll have been over-run, but so what? As Thatcherism teaches us, the dogma is always right; it's the facts which cannot be relied upon.

Mr Rifkind also revealed that we were looking for a new 'sub-strategic capacity' which is jargon for the actual warheads our submarines will fire. Suppose you were at Ground Zero in Baghdad, and looked up to see a cone-shaped warhead drop megatons of unsold copies of *The Downing Street Years*? You would sue for peace immediately and it would be MALCOLMs all round for the flight crew.

19 October 1993

I found Lady Thatcher's memoirs, *The Downing Street Years*, fascinating, but wondered just how much her innumerable American and Japanese admirers would enjoy her immensely detailed accounts of how she beat this strike, or reshaped that industry.

The soi-disant 'Granny' Thatcher is loose again, like Tony Perkins's mother in *Psycho*. With a flash of grey hair, a swirl of skirt, and the screeching of pizzicato violins, she raises her weapon behind her shoulder. Almost before the victim knows what is happening, it has smashed down on the title page and the book is signed.

When John Smith arrived in the Chamber yesterday for the first Prime Minister's Question Time since July, Mr Major smiled warmly across at him. No wonder. Thanks to the new security arrangements at the House (we have turnstiles now in the familiar Commons style of kitsch Gothic, as if obtained at a royal gifte shoppe, a collaboration between Pugin and Ove Arup), this is one place where she might find it hard to get in. He could relax, spread out, be himself for a change.

Yet we all know that mild Tony Perkins and his demented, homicidal mother were really the same person. Is this true of Mr Major? She has announced that she is back in charge. He has not denied this, perhaps because in some way he has actually *become* her. There'll be a good bit at the end of the film when we see his face superimposed on her grinning skull.

Mr Major began in his new granny role. 'I actually believe in prison as a punishment as well as a deterrent! I am far more worried about innocent people being trapped in their homes than I am about the guilty being imprisoned!' he said.

Only towards the end did we get a glimpse of the old John Major, the one which was there before his personality was taken over. A Labour MP asked him about the secret sources of Tory Party funds.

'I will let you in on a secret,' he said. 'There are a great many secret sources and they are all cheese and wine parties up and down the country!'

This was the old Major – the faintly surrealist use of language, the mild obsession with food, and the ability to miss the point altogether. We will miss him, unless medical science finds a way to bring him back.

(Actually there's no need for that, because there is his older brother, Terry Major-Ball, who I had the pleasure of meeting some weeks later. Mr Major-Ball is extraordinarily good-natured, limitlessly courteous, if perhaps somewhat obsessed by detail. For example, he tends to say things like: 'No, I tell a lie, it wasn't the vicar, it was the curate I met ...' Like his brother, he too is interested in food. For example, he described how his family had been poor but happy – then apologized for using the cliché. 'We had nothing in the house except some tomatoes,' he said, 'and some baked beans, and perhaps some bacon and some bread ...'

A colleague who knows him well said that he was vital to an understanding of his little brother. 'Terry is the half of John Major which is kind and thoughtful and generous. He just hasn't got the half which is ambitious and sometimes mean-spirited.')

20 October 1993

**As usual, the Queen opened Parliament at the beginning
of the new legislative year.**

Politicians are obsessed with finding out what ordinary
taxpayers think, so it was fortunate that one of them
turned up yesterday to give them her views on what the
government ought to be doing. Unfortunately, Her
Majesty's speech – it was the first time she had opened
Parliament since the Inland Revenue had got their hooks
in – sounded like something John Major himself might
have written. Which, of course, he largely did.

'My government will work to ensure that the principle
of subsidiarity is applied to European Community
legislation ... the Citizen's Charter will remain central to
my government's programme.' When you are a slightly
stooped, elderly woman in glasses, obliged to read out
these dreary formulae, it is hard to look regal even when
you *are* wearing a crown and gown.

Happily there was a more queenly figure present. It was
Margaret Thatcher's first State Opening as a baroness,
and she looked superb. Swathed in red robes and ermine,
candy floss hair so meticulous that no one would dream of
hiding it under a mere crown, she gazed serenely into the
middle distance. She was as gracious as all get out. Most
politicians are doomed to grow like their *Spitting Image*
puppet. More alarmingly, she is turning into the picture
on the cover of her book.

The State Opening is one of those ancient, unchanged
British political traditions that goes back for months, if
not years. So each time one looks for subtle, minor
changes. For example, these days the post of Cap of
Maintenance is held by Lord Wakeham. (Queen Beatrix
presumably is accompanied by the Dutch Cap of
Maintenance.) 'Cap', as his friends must call him, has the
job of holding up, on a stick, the piece of red cloth which
prevents the crown from slipping off the royal bonce. It

seems an apt task for a man who works as a special adviser to John Major. In any event, he looked as if he had just hooked it off the head of a department store Santa.

Other celebrity peers included the 7th Marquess of Bath, better known as the Loins of Longleat. He sat behind a long line of women, one of whom was wearing an extremely low cut white satin number. Could these all be the famous 'wifelets'? I decided not. These days most peers' wives seem to go in for over the top (or in the case of the woman in white, under the top) dresses in shimmering multi-coloured sequins. They looked like Ladies' Night at the Basildon Masons. Say what you like about Britain, but no other country in the world can put on a ceremony quite as naff as ours.

Back in the Commons, the prime minister responded to a question from John Smith, who wanted to know why, when the *Los Angeles Times* had asked him why things were going wrong for the government, he had replied with the words: 'Fiddle-dee-dee!', suggesting to me once again that Mr Major learned slang from an outdated textbook in a British Council library.

19 November 1993

This is a theory I have held for quite some time and some months ago I wrote an article about it:

I've been wondering why Mr Major's vocabulary is so strange, and have come up with a radical new theory. This occurred to me while listening to his speech in Harrogate last weekend. Apropos unemployment, he declared puzzlingly: 'Fine words butter no parsnips!' Later in his text, he was to say 'drat it!' but changed it to 'damn it!'

These antiquated proverbs and phrases will be familiar to anyone who has spent time in one of our former colonies. The British Council library always contains, along with rows of Dickens and Shakespeare, masses of well thumbed detective stories, plus dusty books with titles such as *Speak English the Way the English Do*. These elderly works generally contain advice such as 'If you wish to tell your British friend that what you do is more important than what you say, tell him: "Fine words butter no parsnips!" ... someone who is very angry indeed may exclaim: "Drat it!" '

My theory is that our prime minister is actually Nigerian. According to his biographies, he went to Nigeria in 1966, to work in the northern town of Jos. I surmise that he was actually born and raised there. The nearest British Council library was in Kaduna, 100 miles away – nothing to a barefoot boy with an unquenchable thirst for knowledge. Here, through the stilted prose of Agatha Christie, he would have learned his famous circumlocutions, such as 'plied his trade in the environs of', for 'worked near'.

This would account for the surprising vagueness about his early life: where he actually lived, how many O Levels he passed, the variable family surname. It would also explain the pronunciation of 'wunt' for 'want' – unknown in Brixton but, I am told, common among the Hausa people.

It might be pointed out that, for someone of African ethnic origin, Mr Major is the wrong colour. To which I reply, look at Michael Jackson.

14 March 1993

Defence questions always bring out the angriest Conservative MPs who want to keep the armed forces exactly as they are.

Mr Nicholas Fairbairn, his nannyish voice like a mountain sheep with flu, wanted the Gordon Highlanders to remain separate from the Queen's Own Highlanders. Mr Nicholas Winterton wished to preserve military bands, fearing a disastrous fall in national morale if they were to go.

Then up stood a tall, ram-rod straight figure with a voice which could have steadied the line at Rorke's Drift. How did this government dare to talk about lack of foresight? No one in the armed forces had any idea of what the future held. (This is true. Uncertainty means that a typical career progression for an army officer is subaltern, captain, major, estate agent.) It was well known, the commanding figure roared, that the ministry of defence kept three sets of statistics: one to deceive the public, one to deceive parliament, and one to deceive itself.

It was only faintly surprising that this gallant display came from Mr John Reid, a Labour spokesman on defence, whose military experience has been limited to the research department of the Scottish Labour Party where he probably encountered more hand-to-hand fighting than most modern soldiers ever do.

But it was a looking-glass day all round. John Smith wanted to know why the prime minister had 'shamelessly betrayed' his promises on taxation.

Mr Major looked triumphant. The leader of the Opposition had a 'very selective memory' he said, if he had forgotten his own plans to raise national insurance contributions.

But the point is that in April 1992 Mr Smith said he would put up taxes, and Mr Major said that his lot wouldn't. That is no doubt why Mr Major won the election and Mr Smith's side did not. It seems perverse, to say the least, to imply that it was Mr Smith who was fibbing.

24 November 1993

I had seen Michael Heseltine speak at a meeting in Newcastle a month or so after the Tory conference. It was his first public speech since his heart attack, and was a muted affair. The man who, in Julian Critchley's famous words, always knew where to find the Conservative Party's clitoris, settled for an amiable slap on the back instead. He told me his doctors had suggested caution: 'You know, the way I speak ...' In late November he returned for his first performance in the Commons.

Mr Heseltine is the only politician I know whose peroration starts in the third sentence. He is ranting by the time most others finish clearing their throat, 0–60 in ten seconds, so to speak. Dennis Skinner shouted: 'I've got a little tablet 'ere yer can put under yer tongue.' But it made no difference. The voice rose, the hair quivered, the arms were first thrust out, then waved around the Chamber and finally set akimbo. The jokes weren't too bad. 'Someone asked me, "How's life?", and I told them, "An awful lot better than the alternative." ' He had a go at John Prescott for wanting, he alleged, to end containerization and have workers carrying their loads round in sacks. 'Then we could have a National Union of Sack Carriers, paying its funds to the Labour Party, with sponsored Sack Carriers' MPs ...'

In an insufferably grey government, Mr Heseltine

stands out like a flash deed in a dreary world. But my pleasure was enhanced by hearing his opposite number, Robin Cook, produce a speech which was every bit as good. He exposed the story about the European Union's alleged 26,911-word directive on caramel as just another Euro-fable, and he derided the Great Campaign of Deregulation by pointing out that, in the past 14 years, *Butterworth's Company Law*, a volume hitherto unknown to me, had expanded from fewer than 500 pages to more than 5,000.

Mr Cook is crisp, witty and penetrating. He is definitely a victim of sizeism in that, if he did not look like a vandalized garden gnome, people would be calling him the next Labour leader.

There is one problem, which he can easily tackle. Mr Cook tends to gabble. And to gobble. He swallows whole strings of syllables so that words slither down his throat like tapeworms. By getting my ear in, and paying close attention to the context, I could translate at least some of what he said. For instance, the 'kiv conc' was the Conservative conference. The 'onul vur' was the honourable member for. The National Consumer Conference was transmogrified into the 'Nashcuckon'.

'The pessage provs thaip in diz' was easy, plainly referring to the percentage of profits they pay in dividends. But the most elegant of the lot, a super-elision which would have brought an appreciative curl to Professor Higgins's lip, was one in which nine long syllables were reduced to four short ones: 'Sinzaydezl' is Cookese for 'since that is always desirable'.

25 November 1993

At the end of November, the chancellor of the exchequer presented the first ever unified, tax 'n' spend Budget.

As he arrived at the front bench, there was no space for Ken Clarke, so he solved that problem by sitting on both the prime minister and the home secretary, one of their haunches beneath each of his cheeks. They moved quickly after that.

The chancellor looked unusually nervous, tapping his fingers on his speech, his head lolling back, swallowing frequently. Then just before he was due to speak, Mr Andrew Faulds stood up on a point of order. Tories started laughing with anticipation.

'Listen, you berks!' Mr Faulds almost screamed. Mr Faulds is the parliamentary equivalent of the All Blacks' *haka*, the Maori war chant which is supposed to strike terror into their opponents. It didn't do the New Zealanders any good last Saturday [they had unexpectedly lost to England at Twickenham] and it didn't achieve much for Mr Faulds either.

Mr Clarke visibly relaxed. He did not so much stand at the Despatch Box as belly up to it, as if about to ask for another pint of Best and a bag of scratchings. He is a curiously apolitical figure, covertly liked by the other lot, who generally prefer to sit back and enjoy his performances. This will bring him little credit with his own party, who tend to be suspicious of leaders who are inadequately detested by the other side.

Mr Clarke's Jack-the-Lad style, the galloping diction which glossed over some points and ignored others altogether, concealed some of the important changes which the Budget is likely to bring about. For example, on student grants: 'Why should the taxpayer finance all the living costs of tomorrow's lawyers?' he asked cheerily. Well, so that a pitman's son could attend Cambridge in the first place, train as a lawyer and go on to be chancellor of the exchequer, perhaps.

Or the new £28 child care allowance, introduced so that mothers can go out to work. But there are too few jobs. What will they do? Become child minders, of course. It's another example of the way that the British economy is coming to resemble the island invented by Lewis Carroll in *Sylvie and Bruno* where the inhabitants scratch a living by taking in each other's washing.

Or the intriguing new Venture Capital Trust, which will allow people to make tax-free investments in small businesses. How small? Those smelly vans in laybys saying 'Look! Tea, Burgers', or chaps who sell over-priced ovengloves from door to door? In the undergrowth of the economy, the eco-system changes at bewildering speed, especially with the government's help.

We also learned of some cunning neologisms coined by ministers to make their changes more acceptable. The old sickness and invalidity benefits have been run together and renamed 'incapacity benefit'. A small verbal tweak, to be sure, but doesn't 'incapable' sound subtly worse than merely sick, or invalid? 'Pull yourself together, man, you're not incapable!'

Similarly the unemployed are now renamed 'jobseekers', entitled to the 'Jobseekers' Allowance' provided they first sign a 'Jobseekers' Agreement'. This is a more potent switch. Imagine one of those gloomy newsreaders who disagree with Martyn Lewis about the good news, intoning that 'the number of jobseekers rose again last month'. It sounds too positive, too perky. Instead of malingerers in grubby vests drinking beer in front of the TV, we are asked to see an army of bright-eyed youngsters venturing forth to see if Burger King are hiring.

My favourite is the new name for cuts in higher education grants. This is now known as 'expanding loan entitlement', rather like unemployment could have been called 'expanding leisure entitlement', except that it's called 'jobseeking' instead.

This was a harsh Budget but delivered with enough flair and good humour to please the Tories and, at first, leave the Labour benches uneasily quiet. Mr Smith had little choice but to take the opposite tack and deliver a furious partisan denunciation, such as we hadn't seen from him for months.

'Odious ... my stomach turned ... this vicious attack on the welfare state ... a party which, when it needs money, turns on the sick and unemployed ...'

It made me nostalgic for the days when the Labour Party not only cared about social justice, but was prepared to say so, very loudly if necessary.

Mr Smith looked furious. Mr Clarke even looked embarrassed. But all was well. As soon as Smith sat down, the prime minister passed him a note. Smith waved in friendly acknowledgement, and Major waved back. That's Parliament; a gentleman's club in which the members are invited to scream at each other across the Reading Room.

(Mr Smith later told me that the note had been an apology from the PM for a remark he'd made earlier which had sounded more insulting than he'd meant. *Quelle delicatesse!*)

1 December 1993

Towards the end of the year the Chinese government, with a great show of anger, rejected Governor Chris Patten's proposals for the future of the Hong Kong legislative council and broke off the various continuing talks with the British. This caused some excitement back at Westminster, though perhaps predictably it turned out to be another Oriental ploy, no doubt connected with the imminent death of Supreme Leader Deng Xiaoping. Soon after this debate, Deng was seen on Chinese television, doddering forward on the arms of his daughters, drooling and grinning foolishly. This was either designed to prove to the Chinese people that he was still alive, or to warn them of his moribund state. Or possibly both.

The problem of Hong Kong, and what will happen in 1997, is one which always unites the House of Commons in a morose sense of impotence. How can you conduct negotiations when one of the countries involved has recently become a hotbed of uncontrolled capitalism, yet is still ruled by a ferociously autocratic government, wedded to a long discredited dogma? To make the job even tougher, the nominal premier can hardly speak for himself, being under the sway of a semi-gaga former leader whose slightest whim remains law.

Granted, some people would find this an exaggerated description of Britain today, and particularly of Lady Thatcher's role. After all, former Chairman Deng, who runs China from what will no doubt be his deathbed, at least has the official title of President of the All-China Bridge Federation. Lady Thatcher does not even have that bauble.

(She does, however, have the equivalent of a *Little Red Book* in the form of her memoirs. Unhappily, at 914 pages, this is not a handy size for waving at mass rallies, show trials etc. Perhaps they will produce a condensed version, containing her Thoughts in suitably compact form. 'That Geoffrey Howe – ugh! Chancellor Kohl – disgustingly fat! Nigel Lawson – oh, puh-leeze!')

Traditionally Britain has dealt with China in two ways: either we sent a gunboat to grab what we wanted, e.g. Hong Kong. Or else we grovelled to whichever tyrant happened to be in power at the time.

Neither of these is Douglas Hurd's style. He is, after all, a mandarin himself who has, as he has told David Frost, no more ambitions to be anything else. His tone yesterday was chatty yet rueful, no more bellicose or grovelling than any other Old Etonian foreign secretary. The Chinese, he explained patiently if a little wearily, had had 'no difficulty of principle ... proposals largely uncontroversial in Hong Kong ... we had thought they were uncontroversial with China ...' He didn't actually say 'inscrutable, these Chinese' – he is far too sophisticated – but that was the tone. Not even a threat to give them a taste of cold draft proposals.

Various MPs rose to ask what was going on. Mr Hurd continued to express gentlemanly regret. Only one question aroused any emotion. Mr David Harris, the Tory MP for St Ives, said that he was just back from 'Beijing'. The foreign secretary snorted. 'It is a matter of personal taste [one of those remarks people use when they mean the opposite] but I for one don't go round saying "Roma" or "Bruxelles" or "Moskva". Why should people abandon that perfectly good word "Peking"?'

He was loudly applauded for this. I agree. In fact, we should go further, and insist on English back-formations for all foreign place names. So we would visit 'Pleasant Breezes' in Argentina, 'Black Pool', the capital of Ireland, and Disneyland in 'The Angels'. San Francisco would be more conveniently known as 'Frank'.

(Shortly after this debate I returned to Hong Kong, where I learned two curious things. The first is that officials from

Her Majesty's Treasury still arrive in the colony to explain to the government where it has gone wrong, a practice which has survived the fact that Hong Kong recently passed the United Kingdom, Australia and Canada in per capita income.

I was also shown the Queen's suite at Government House. The bathroom there has recently been refurbished, and the mahogany toilet seat and lid fitted with highly polished brass rings on the side, so that the royal digits need not be sullied by touching the wood where others' bare bottoms have sat. It seemed a fitting symbol of the end of Empire, rather like Ozymandias's trunkless legs of stone.)

                                                    7 December 1993

Shortly before Christmas, MPs debated Sunday trading hours. Things got off to a loopy start.

Sir Peter Hordern is one of a dwindling band of survivors from the once mighty herd that roamed the Commons: the Knights of the Shires. His intention was to help small shopkeepers, making him a Knight of the Spars.

He also wanted to recognize, as he put it, 'that the greatness of Great Britain has been based on an Anglo-Saxon, Celtic, Christian philosophy. People who believe in that may be a minority but they have a right to be listened to.' (Or obeyed, which I suspect is what he meant.)

His plan was to Keep Sunday Semi-Special. Shops could open only after 1 pm, so people could go to church – the Knight of the Spires. Or rather, some shops would be allowed to open in the mornings too, but only to sell

Sunday newspapers (not books, Bibles or Slush Puppies) or pharmaceuticals (but not condoms or bath oils). Cafés, restaurants, airport shops and garden centres could all open too.

In other words, he was offering a dog's breakfast, except that dog food would not be available till lunchtime either. With his orotund manner and his evocation of our nation's past glories, Sir Peter is easy to laugh at, so MPs did. They delightedly exposed the absurdities. Someone asked about gifte shoppes in stately homes. Yes, he said, they too would have to remain closed until 1 pm. But he added, as if this made it all right, he had been able to assure a peer of his acquaintance that this meant he would get the chance to stay in bed longer.

Perhaps he was referring to the Marquess of Bath, famous for his 'wifelets', who needs all the extra sack time he can get.

Someone asked why it was all right for people to read papers or do the gardening on a Sunday morning, but not to eat.

'They can eat in a restaurant!' Sir Peter reminded them, impatiently. The Tories erupted in mirth. Didn't he know that Wilton's is closed on a Sunday lunchtime?

Next was Mr Peter Pike, the Labour member for Burnley, who spoke against the deregulation of shopping hours. With his crinkly hair and twinkling eyes behind half-moon glasses, Mr Pike looks exactly like one of those old-fashioned shopkeepers who believe in personal service and who are disappearing so fast from our towns and villages.

Thank goodness, as I sometimes churlishly think while waiting to buy a pint of milk behind a particularly loquacious gossip. Similarly, Mr Pike kept strolling off down Memory Lane, or Memory Access Road as it has been renamed. Suddenly he was talking about a sausage shop in Clitheroe. Then he recalled that he had just had a letter from a vicar. Not any old vicar, either, but the vicar of the church where he, Mr Pike, had been married on this very day, 31 years ago!

Finally he finished, and Dame Angela Rumbold rose. She's a toughie. She'd put in her order, and get out of the shop. But we had no such luck. Why, she mused, that church was in her own constituency, and what a very beautiful church it was! She congratulated Mr Pike on his anniversary and cordially wished him another 31 equally happy years.

At this point I began to wish for one of the glossy new market-driven chain MPs to drive the 'little man' out of business. Worst of all, these days you can turn on the TV at almost any time on the Sabbath and watch MPs engaged in Sunday trading themselves on the innumerable political shows. I keep Sunday special myself by leaving the set off.

9 December 1993

Whenever the prime minister misses his own Question Time, his place is taken by the Leader of the House, Mr Tony Newton.

Mr Newton is widely liked but not for his devil-may-care candour. Ask him if he'd like a drink, and he would say: 'I don't think I would be straying too far outside my remit, or indeed telling you anything you perhaps don't already know, but a glass of dry white wine would be most acceptable – that is off the record, of course.' Ask him the time, and he'd need to ring an official to make sure Big Ben confirmed it publicly. He would then worry that he might have given away too much.

However, put him at the Despatch Box and he instantly becomes a snarling tiger of anti-socialist rhetoric, a Heseltine without the hair. Yesterday he was helped in his task by a fine crop of planted questions from oleaginous Tory MPs who were hoping for preferment through obsequiousness. Some of them, I fear, will one day melt into a pool of butter, like the tiger which pursued Little Black Sambo.

For instance, Dr Ian Twinn, the Tory member for Edmonton, reminded him glutinously that the Japanese ambassador had recently described Britain as a 'trailblazer' for European investment.

Mr Newton was able, on the instant, to add more of his excellency's encomium. I make no comment myself, except to point out that a wise ambassador lies not only on behalf of his own country, but for his host nation as well.

Mrs Margaret Beckett then accused Mr Newton of using procedural tactics to 'run away' from a vote on VAT on domestic fuel. This is one of those intramural matters which Labour MPs seem to imagine will, if they bore on long enough, deliver the electorate into their hands. I shall believe it when I hear a candidate being told on the doorstep: 'Blimey, vote for your lot after you lumped VAT on domestic fuel in with other Budget provisions, pursuant to paragraph 3 of Standing Order 50? Stroll on!'

The loudest fake laughter at Mrs Beckett came from Mr Nicholas Soames, the junior agriculture minister, who looked as if he were about to explode, like a mad cow suffering from a hazardous build-up of methane.

Mr Soames is a former equerry to the Prince of Wales, and has been widely quoted this week as saying that he had no doubt that the Prince would one day become King.

Which is all well and good. But what about the constitutional position of Mr Soames? He too comes from one of England's great dynasties, even grander perhaps than the Mountbatten-Windsors. He too was born knowing that it was his destiny, perhaps his fate, to rule over us.

He has also suffered the pain of a failed marriage, and has seen his public work overshadowed by an ambitious woman skilled in the arts of media manipulation (Gillian Shephard, his boss).

But is Mr Soames truly fit to rule? The nation is divided. As so often at these crossroads of history, we turn for guidance to the Church.

The Archdeacon of York said (or might have done, if I had asked him): 'Here is a man who has woken up innumerable times and vowed: "I'll never touch another drop", and then that very night has been seen drinking bumpers of claret in White's Club.

'Can we trust a man who breaks his word thus not to betray his Privy Counsellor's oaths as well?'

As a final humiliation, Mr Soames has had to watch himself devastatingly caricatured by a skilful actor in a popular weekend television series.

Even the pink spotted costume is cruelly modelled on his tie; the fact that Mr Blobby is much slimmer fools no one at all.

10 December 1993

In December 1993, Mr Major and the Irish Prime
Minister Albert Reynolds signed the Downing Street
Declaration. This accord was supposed to offer an
ending to the disturbances which have been continuing
in that part of the world for around 25 years. I have
always suspected that the fact they have lasted for a
quarter of a century implies that they have reached an
equilibrium of sorts and that for many people there is no
real or urgent reason why they should end. The violence
has become institutionalized. But that does not stop
prime ministers from attempting yet more initiatives.

It was by any standards a day of awesome historic
significance. Whether it will be remembered next month
is another matter. We old cynics tend to regard solutions
to the Northern Ireland problem as rather like Frank
Sinatra's retirement – always welcome, but we'll believe it
when it happens.

One of Willie Whitelaw's civil servants once said, back
in the mists of history, 'We are always on the brink of the
abyss. But the Irish keep moving the abyss.' In the same
way, we are always on the brink of peace.

The day began with the traditional exchange of
bromides. Mr Major said at Downing Street that the Irish
should not look back to their history, but forwards to
their future. (Unlike us British, of course, who never look
back at the past.) Mr Reynolds pointed out that violence
was always futile, which is one of those remarks everyone
feels obliged to agree with, even though we know it's not
true.

Over at the Commons, the Declaration was received
with rapture by all sides – all, apart from most of the MPs
who will have to live with it.

'A new beginning,' said Peter Temple-Morris. Alan
Beith offered 'sincere and heartfelt goodwill'. It began to
sound like a retirement party. Doug Hoyle mused that
now was the time 'to give peace a chance'.

One reflected how easy it would be to bring about world peace if it were only a matter of various *bien pensants* getting round a mahogany table and agreeing with each other.

And when the House of Commons agrees with itself, it is usually wrong. This phenomenon generally means that someone has found a new way of dodging the problem.

Yesterday that problem was personified by Ian Paisley, who called the Declaration 'a sell-out and an act of treachery'. Mr Paisley has made a long and prosperous career out of never underestimating the intransigence of the Ulster Protestant. He cannot be ignored.

One of the few mainland Tories who seemed remotely sceptical was Nicholas Budgen of Wolverhampton. He was also one of the few who had, perhaps, read the document, and in particular the peculiar statement that Britain has 'no selfish strategic or economic interest in Northern Ireland'.

'Does the government,' Mr Budgen asked innocently, 'still have a selfish strategic and economic interest in Wolverhampton?'

Of course this begged the question: no one imagines that 40 per cent of the people of Wolverhampton would prefer to live under another jurisdiction (such as Walsall). On the other hand, the implicit meaning of the Declaration's terminology was 'We don't want to lose you, but we think you ought to go.' The prime minister was taken aback.

'Don't tempt me,' he said mysteriously, before finding another pro forma reply on a bit of paper.

Henry Bellingham offered the pleasant if eccentric thought that matters could be improved by having an all-Ireland association football team.

Mr Major thought that would be a bad idea, since it would end the exciting Ulster *v.* Republic of Ireland matches. As a fan of Five Nations rugby too, he would also miss that particular clash.

As it happens, there is an all-Ireland rugby team, and

always has been. As a fan, Mr Major might have been expected to know that. But then the British have never understood Ireland.

16 December 1993

> Over the New Year, Mr Major's line in his conference speech about 'back to basics' caused him apparently unending embarrassment. It turned out that the junior minister Tim Yeo had fathered an illegitimate daughter by a Tory councillor in East London. Another had, without actually breaking the law, made a most advantageous house purchase from Westminster Council.

As so often, it was Jeffrey Archer who spoke for us all. 'If we are going to have in public life those people who have an utterly clean sheet, we will end up with people who are not actually capable of governing the country!'

Something of a hostage to fortune, I felt, especially the last part. On the other hand, the bit about clean sheets must have struck a chord with David Ashby, the Tory MP who went on a gastronomic seafood tour of France and wound up in bed with his male travelling companion, a doctor.

Mr Ashby's lawyer, Peter Carter-Ruck, has assured us that nothing untoward took place while they were tucked up with each other, so we may be certain nothing did.

Instead, I picture them as if in those old Morecambe and Wise sketches, sitting up in fleecy pyjamas and eating crisps – except that they would have been munching a mussel, or nibbling on a langoustine, or whatever gastronomes do in bed together. Let's hope they kept dobs of mayonnaise off the duvet!

The other interesting implication of Lord Archer's remarks is that people who have the whiff of scandal about them, rather as a certain type of old-fashioned Tory used to smell of bay rum, are actually better ministers than the goody goodies.

It's the excuses following the various revelations which make me particularly glum. For instance, Mr Ashby said that he had booked a room for two purely in order to save money – a depressingly Thatcherite reason for wanting to go to bed with anyone.

After watching ministers flail around, I returned to the cafeteria for some hot buttered crumpets. A colleague asked me if this was wise in the present climate. Perhaps not. I should have gone back to biscuits.

12 January 1994

In mid-January, the Westminster district auditor published a report on the local council, which he accused of illegally spending millions of pounds of ratepayers' money in order to guarantee its own re-election.

The prime minister yesterday unreservedly condemned the disgraceful behaviour of senior Conservatives who had been caught using millions of pounds of public money to ensure their own re-election.

Well, no, of course he didn't. Just my little pleasantry. Sorry. What he actually said was that the district auditor's findings about Lady Dame Porter – or Dame Lady Mrs Whatever; she collects titles as fast as she boards up council houses – were only 'provisional'. He added at Question Time: 'I think you should wait until those findings are confirmed before you are so quick to judge.'

Quick to judge? It took the auditor the best part of five years to decide that the Dame Lady and her gang had been 'disgraceful and improper' and guilty of 'wilful misconduct'. But, as the prime minister pointed out, this judgement was only 'provisional'.

It called to mind other examples of great parliamentary invective. Denis Healey's assault on Geoffrey Howe: 'like being provisionally savaged by a dead sheep'. Or Leo Amery turning the course of history in the Norway debate: 'In the name of God, go – at least provisionally.'

Certainly, Mr Major has never been guilty of unfair and hasty judgements on Westminster Council. Back in 1991, some 18 months after the auditor had begun his inquiry, he told MPs that Westminster was 'an example to other authorities. I hope they will follow that example.'

Yesterday he – and later his environment secretary, John Gummer – tried to imply that it was Labour which was guilty of moral misconduct for condemning the Lady Dame on the flimsy basis of a four-year inquiry and a mere 10,000 pages of evidence.

'Unlike you,' Mr Major told Mr Smith, 'most people will prefer to wait … and not find people guilty until and unless they are proven to be guilty.'

Clearly the tactic is to hope the thing can be kept off the boil until after the next election, or even the next millennium. Which is why the Tories' more sycophantic back benchers (one would never call them anything as vulgar as 'bum-suckers'; 'langoustine lickers', perhaps) made a mistake in returning so quickly back to basics.

Mr Stephen Milligan (C Eastleigh), who cannot bear for a Question Time to go by without oiling up to somebody, found a way to accuse the Labour Party of breaking up MPs' marriages by keeping them late at the House. Mr Milligan is an old and valued colleague of mine, but I regret to say that he has become typical of the

new, classless Tory Party, being born with a greasy spoon
in his mouth.

14 January 1994

It was exactly 4.29 pm when Mr Ian Lang, the Scottish
secretary, said it. At the end of a long, much interrupted
and necessarily defensive speech about Scottish local
government, he decided to close with a stirring
peroration, a battle cry for his back benchers to stitch into
their banners, something to put a bit of lead in their
cabers.

'We want,' he declared, 'to get back to basics!'

There was a brief silence, perhaps a nano-second
(defined as the period between the light turning green and
the idiot in the Escort GTi behind you blowing his horn)
while the Labour benches absorbed this remark. Then
they erupted in a single gigantic, gleeful, delirious shout.
The rafters shook and the welkin rang. It was, for
Labour, a rare moment of pure distilled joy.

The party's pleasure was heightened by the fact that the
Local Government (Scotland) Bill goes back to the basics
of the eighteenth century. It is probably the most
ambitious piece of gerrymandering attempted by any
British government since the passage of the Reform Act.

It appears to have an ecological function, being
designed to preserve the few remaining examples of the
Scottish Tory, a breed as seriously threatened as the
golden eagle.

The bill replaces the old two-tier system with a
single layer of 28 new councils. When these are likely to
be Labour controlled, they are vast and sprawling. But
where there is a small breeding colony of Tories they are

small, carefully defined and jealously preserved.

Take West Renfrew – population 265,000 – which is to be separated by fretsaw from Tory East Renfrew, with its 88,000 citizens. Whereas the boundaries of some new councils are described in a single phrase, East Renfrew requires some 49 lines in the bill. It's worth quoting at length because it is a rare chance to see what that fabled creature, the gerrymander, actually looks like close up:

'... including those parts of polling districts PS28 in Paisley Abercorn and PS14 (in Strathclyde electoral division 77 (Paisley Central)) lying to the south and east of a line beginning on the White Cart water and running southwards along the Oldbar Burn to the eastern curtilages [curtilages are grounds, not what footballers tear] of Nos 39-41 Ben More Drive ... passing to the east of the property known as The Bungalow, then south-westwards and westwards along the eastern and southern perimeter of Hawkhead House Farm to No 43 Ben Lui Drive, Nos 52 and 50 Ben Wyvis Drive ... then crossing the dismantled railway line ... along the road to its junction with the path leading to Glenapp Road ...'

The effect of this list is richly comic, which is why Mr George Robertson, the shadow Scottish secretary, was able to suggest that Mr Lang 'should ring up the inhabitants of numbers 52 and 50 Ben Wyvis Drive to make sure they vote the right way, so that if necessary the appropriate amendment can be made.'

18 January 1994

> Another example of the prime minister's dark side appeared in January when he gave a dinner for his departing press secretary, the popular Gus O'Donnell. During the festivities he was heard to say of his right-wing MPs, 'I'll fucking crucify them.' His staff denied that he had used those words; the papers which printed them maintained that he had.

Experts on the British constitution often point to the disparity in our bi-cameral system. On the one hand, we have a lively, vigorous chamber, keenly in touch with the lives of ordinary people. On the other, there is a collection of time-serving has-beens, hamstrung by antiquated procedure, droning sleepily on about nothing of importance – or the House of Commons, as it's known.

Yesterday the contrast was marked. The Lords, with great gusto, were slicing up the Government's Police and Magistrates Courts Bill. To paraphrase them, this ghastly legislation would destroy the present magistrates system, and harm the police by putting a political commissar – or chairman of the police authority, to be named by the home secretary – in charge of every force.

'Chilling', and 'a grave danger to independence' said one typical peer, and that was the Lord Chief Justice. Others were less restrained. The most damaging was Willie Whitelaw, a former home secretary, and perhaps the most loyal Conservative who has ever lived.

'I wonder,' he pondered, 'if my honourable and noble friend could explain this major change in the whole history of policing ... far be it from me to be difficult and tiresome, but I must speak out ... sometimes one simply asks: "I wonder why?" '

Us veteran Willie-watchers know what it means when he goes into his 'I'm just a simple country squire', or Jorrocks routine. The measure was, he said, 'very dangerous indeed', which on the Richter scale of Willieisms is around the level of Krakatoa erupting.

Back in the Neverland of the Commons, the prime minister was making his first appearance since the 'fucking crucify them' imbroglio. It is said that the source for the remarks was indirectly Mr Michael Brunson of ITN, who was seen talking to the prime minister on the night in question. I have no idea whether or not this is true, but I do know that Mr Brunson is hard of hearing in one ear. Perhaps Mr Major had actually said something quite different.

Does he think that Mr Portillo is being held back by his peculiar looks? 'I'll flipping beautify him,' he may have said. Or that the diligent Mr Redwood was hoping for a better job than Wales? 'I'll luckily satisfy him.'

Or it could have been more complicated. Had the agriculture minister Gillian Shephard been avoiding the crisis of insect pests in Britain's orchards? That would be 'ducking fruit fly'.

Over in the more important House, Jim Callaghan was blaming the government for the law and order problem. He accused young Tory ministers of 'flitting from department to department, sucking the honey until the bees kick them out'.

Or 'sucking butterflies', as the prime minister may have told Mr Brunson.

19 January 1994

In January we were finally told some of the government's plans for the new rail link with the Channel Tunnel.

The French end of the Channel Tunnel rail link being long since completed, the government has decided to do something about the British bit. Mr MacGregor, the transport secretary, announced the plans in the Commons. Trains will travel at 185 mph from Paris, then zip through the Tunnel to Folkestone, where passengers will transfer to ox wagons.

No, just a drollery! In fact, they will still be on trains, but not on horrid, modern, continental trains. Instead they will be like the trains drawn by the late Rowland Emmett, with kettles instead of funnels and birds nesting in the cab. They will putter slowly past hedgerows, duckponds, rickety old signal boxes and level crossings manned by ragamuffin boys in baggy shorts and caps.

How dull and utilitarian the TGV will seem as the British train meanders past villages called (these are all near the route) Snodland, Dad Street, Pratt's Bottom, Smeeth, and Grafty Green. Is there anyone so soulless that they would wish to rush through Swingfield Minnis, Stalling Minnis, and – especially – Loose? Or Hucking, Plucking and Fawkham Green, as in the prime minister's words, 'I'll Hucking crucify them'?

One decision the government has made is that the London terminal will be at St Pancras. It is the perfect choice: magnificently ornate, supremely impractical, evocative of a long vanished age. But, if they were looking for a mock-Gothic palace to remind foreigners of Britain's past glories, why couldn't they choose the Houses of Parliament? They would make the finest rail terminal in the world. MPs could move to a shed in Chalk Farm.

Next, the House switched to the Incapacity for Work Bill, which is meant to make it harder for people to claim incapacity benefit. The government has come up with a complicated series of 76 tests, eg 'has difficulty using scissors'. You score points for failing, and if you get above 15 points in any one section, then you are thought incapable of work and can claim the benefit.

As Mr Lilley droned on – I find his earnest, high-pitched voice, like a peeved rabbit, pleasantly soporific – my eye strayed to the tests themselves. They are somewhat unnerving. Test 4: finds it difficult to stir himself to do things, scores 4 points. Test 3: loses track of conversations regularly is 11 points. That brings me up to 15 already, and we haven't even looked at the Mental Health Impairment Score: 'Do you need someone to encourage you to get up and dressed?' 'Are there frequently so many things to do that you just give up?'

But that is nothing to the problems faced by the prime minister. 'Frequently confused or muddled' scores him 23.5 right away. Add 'speech cannot be understood by strangers' for 17, and 'unable to choose between balanced arguments and give a reason for the choice' with a bonus of 4.5, and he should be on triple benefit already.

25 January 1994

Bafflingly, Dame Barbara Cartland claimed in January to be a frequent adviser of the prime minister.

As I arrived at the Commons the result of the Gillian Taylforth case had just become known. A colleague felt she had brought much unwelcome publicity upon herself. 'She should have kept her head down,' he said.

This on a day when we learned that one of Mr Major's principal advisers, the one who claims to have persuaded him to launch the back to basics campaign, was Dame Barbara Cartland. Impossible, we thought. And yet, and yet …

As he arrived in the Chamber, Ginny Bottomley flashed a comforting grin at him. Good old Ginny, what a sport she was! He felt steadier now, sure of himself, certain he would make short work of the cads on the other side.

Beith rose – Alan Beith, the Liberal spokesman whose saturnine good looks and cruel scowl had made him feared throughout Westminster. At the time of the last election, he said with a cruel leer, the government had known it would have to raise taxes because of the £28 billion deficit. 'Or did this important fact escape your notice?' he sneered, cruelly.

The House held its breath in awe. No one dared impugn John Major's honour and expect to escape unscathed. A light smile played about his lips.

'If I had expected to have had to raise taxes after the election, I would not have expressed the contrary view.'

The snivelling Beith cowered in shame and confusion, impaled on the rapier of his own cruel scorn.

Then Margaret Beckett rose. How lovely she looked, with her lustrous flaxen hair atop a lustrous blue jacket which accentuated her soft, womanly figure. Why had a cruel fate so cruelly stranded them on opposite banks of the swirling river of politics?

Oh dear, perhaps not. But the session did give the prime minister the opportunity to road test his new defence to the accusation of lying to the electorate over taxes. Raising them 'was not an easy decision. Not one we would have wished to take. But it was the right decision, and governments cannot duck the right decision.'

This was expanded by Mr Portillo, who spoke about VAT on fuel. Fittingly for someone whose middle name is Xavier, Mr Portillo took a Jesuit approach. Jesuits devote themselves to finding a rational explanation for irrational faith, which is a fair description of most Tory right-wingers.

His line was that the government's fibs over tax actually allowed it to claim the moral high ground. 'Governments have to cope with the circumstances they find, and if they are good governments, they do it according to their principles! We gave a solemn pledge that we would deliver sound public finances! We have principles!'

This is not logic that has been chopped so much as whizzed through a Cuisinart. Earlier Tam Dalyell had risen on a point of order to complain, somewhat lengthily and ponderously, that he had not been invited to the grand launch of the government's new policy on the environment. It seemed a waste of time; as Mr Portillo would certainly have told him, there is no such thing as a free launch.

(Mr Beith does have a curious effect on some of his colleagues, even though he is the most courteous of men, who, for example, never omits to inform other MPs when he visits their constituencies. For months Sir Clement Freud kept up the amusing fantasy that Beith was the Yorkshire Ripper, and would demonstrate how, whenever the Ripper struck, Beith was absent from the division lobbies. Told that a court would need more evidence, Freud replied: 'have you seen the way he walks?'

Others made the point that it could not possibly be Beith, since each time he committed a murder he would have felt obliged to write a letter to the MP in whose constituency he had done it.)

26 January 1994

Agriculture Questions could be surprisingly heated.

The parliamentary day began with a disgraceful attack on one respected public figure. During Agriculture Questions, David Evans (C Welwyn, Hatfield) announced that his wife, whose name is Janice, had told him that the average British family paid an extra £28 a week to support the Common Agricultural Policy.

Normally one would disregard what Mr Evans says about anything, on the grounds that he is a loud-mouthed know-nothing who makes Norman Tebbit look like Brian Sewell. On the other hand, he has just been elected to the Executive of the 1922 Committee and so, in the fantastical dream world of modern British politics, is someone whom we must now take seriously.

Mr Evans wanted Mrs Shephard, the agriculture secretary, to say ('say' is perhaps an inadequate way of describing Mr Evans's own style of speech. 'Bellow' would be more accurate. I have put the words which he shouted in capitals):

'Whevver you agree wiv JANICE that if the WRIGGLER from MONKLANDS [believed to be a reference to John Smith] or the ROMEO from YEOVIL [Mr Jeremy 'Paddy' Ashdown, LibDem, Yeovil] EVER got their hands on the Brussels European chequebook, then the 80 pahnd a week each family is be'er off after 14 years of CONSERVATIVE gummt would disappear like RATS darn a DRAINPIPE!'

What a cheap and sleazy attack. There's something wretchedly sordid about comparing Mr Ashdown to Romeo, so dragging up an event which happened a long time ago and which most people believed was now closed.

For unlike Mr Ashdown, Romeo was famous for his fidelity. He did not say: 'But, soft, what light through yonder window breaks?/It is my secretary, who is working late.'

Furthermore, Romeo is in no position to reply, being dead. It is all too sadly typical of the modern Conservative Party that they should dig up dirt against one of the nation's best-loved fictional characters for their own puny political purposes.

28 January 1994

The Speaker rose to address Parliament on a matter of the gravest importance. It concerned the emblem of the House of Commons, which might look like a flaming waffle to you, but is in fact a 'crown portcullis'. The symbol embodies the dignity of Parliament, and thus perhaps of democracy itself, which is why Ms Boothroyd was so very cross to see it displayed on the cover of Edwina Currie's new novel about the cut and thrust of politics (especially the thrust), *A Parliamentary Affair*.

The sacred symbol, the Commons' equivalent of Mickey Mouse's ears, is depicted on the heel of a stocking which encases a long female leg. The Speaker was so vexed about this, I am told, that she privately gave Mrs Currie a heated telling-off.

But yesterday Edwina was not to be seen. 'Where is she?' MPs growled. As it happens, she was signing books in Birmingham, but those who have read her *oeuvre* tend to be suspicious of what she might be up to when she is not in plain sight (though I should point out that Commons offices have no locks, which must have given her characters an extra frisson).

I rushed out to buy a copy, but the booksellers told me that it has been so popular they could not obtain supplies [it sold 49,000 in hardback]. So I did what any hack worth his salt would do and made it up:

Edwina gazed at herself in the mirror, admiring the pert, upthrusting nose, and the moist, red, receptive mouth. Not bad for 47 she thought, not bad at all. It was lucky that the camera adored her figure, lissom and buxom at the same time, because she adored publicity, needed it, could never get enough of it. And she did not mind who gave it to her, just as long as they kept it coming, strong and hard.

The phone rang. A seductive, lilting voice was on the line.

'It is Colwyn Bay Hospital Radio here, Mrs Currie. Sorry to bother you, but we wondered whether you could

take part in a three-minute discussion …'

Her lips parted, and her voice was husky, distant, barely able to coax a sound from her tightened larynx. 'Yes, yes, yes!' she managed to cry.

'How will you get here?' the man asked.

'You'll have to take me, take me!' she moaned, as rhythmic, uncontrollable emotions pulsed through her arching body.

Then she balanced the smallest strawberry gently on his very bobbit tip, where it wobbled dangerously. After a thoughtful pause, she covered it with a whirl of cream. 'I have always wanted to eat you, Roger Dickson.'

'Elaine, careful with your teeth, I cannot get a replacement,' he said.

I have cheated, since the last two paragraphs are actual quotes from the book, except that Edwina does not use the word bobbit.

Ms Boothroyd said that it was one of her principal duties to uphold the dignity of the House. 'I hope I have made abundantly clear the importance I attach to this matter.'

No doubt Edwina, whose political career is now wobbling as dangerously as her hero's strawberry, will be quietly delighted by all this publicity – insofar as she is quietly delighted by anything.

(Mrs Currie had made no secret of her view that she felt the political future lay in Europe, and in June 1994 ran in the Conservative cause for a seat centred on Milton Keynes. She lost by quite a hefty margin, variously attributed to the publicity around this book, to her stand on the homosexual age of consent, but which in fact probably was the result of the swing against her party.)

1 February 1994

The Pergau Dam scandal, in which the government was accused of paying for an unwanted dam in Malaysia in exchange for valuable arms contracts, emerged in January, thanks to the honesty and courage of a senior civil servant, Sir Tim Lankester.

The Commons foreign affairs committee is not famed for the ferocity of its grilling. You'll have seen tougher interrogations by Paula Yates on the Big Breakfast bed.

However, the committee did interview Douglas Hurd on the Pergau Dam, and if they didn't exactly shake him, they did contrive to rattle his cage, an achievement in itself.

The foreign secretary opened with the Grandee's Defence, or the GD as we old hands call it. These were matters which, he implied, might excite lesser mortals. There had been a 'swirl' of speculative allegations. Some had even linked the affair with contributions to Conservative Party funds! Such claims were 'creatures of fancy' (one of those orotund phrases which I tend to translate as 'probably true').

He was sure that the committee's proceedings would lay these preconceptions to rest. They had been 'written a long way from the real world in which Britain has to exist'.

This is the core of the classic GD. Britain's behaviour is invariably beyond reproach, except when it isn't. This is always because we have to live in the real world, which is regrettably full of foreigners.

The GD then moves on to tackle the grandee's accusers, by magnanimously forgiving them. In this case it was Sir Tim Lankester. 'I have no criticism of the way Sir Tim has handled this matter, but I had to take a wider perspective ...' Mr Hurd said, in the manner of one pardoning a butler who had spilled gravy in a guest's lap.

At around this point a well spoken black man stood up in the public seats and shouted 'Douglas Hurd is a liar and a cheat!' The House of Commons is the last habitat of the traditional, twinkle-eyed British bobby; three of them dragged him away and chucked him into the corridor.

Utterly unflapped, Mr Hurd continued on his courteous but faintly weary way, occasionally deferring on finer points to an official, a Mr Manning, who looked disconcertingly like Oddjob with a wasting disease.

The whole thing, you felt, had been got up by the irresponsible muckrakers of the Civil Service. In 1988, Sir George Younger, who was then our defence secretary, had signed a protocol in Kuala Lumpur which appeared to make our arms sales depend on the supply of aid, something which was against declared government policy.

'We took early action to make clear to the Malaysians that the linkage was not possible,' Mr Hurd said, plonkingly. The committee's collective nostrils began to quiver. Had the High Commissioner, who attended these negotiations, not been aware that it was all terribly wrong?

Mr Hurd took refuge in that convenient bolt-hole, the real world. There had been no time for leisurely consideration. The government was at risk of losing the whole agreement.

It then turned out that on the very day that the Malaysian government learned that the link between arms and aid was to be cancelled, it received another letter saying that aid would continue to flow as before. The very same day!

The committee snorted. 'You said to Malaysia that we'd made a bit of a lash-up, but don't worry,' said David Harris (C St Ives) scornfully. 'It strains credulity,' said someone else. 'Extraordinary, is it not?' inquired another.

This is the committee's elliptical way of echoing what the young black heckler had shouted: 'Douglas Hurd is a liar and a cheat!'

3 February 1994

**In early February we learned of the death of Stephen
Milligan, the Conservative MP for Eastleigh, who had
asphyxiated himself while 'engaged in an act of
auto-eroticism', as the stuffier papers put it. I had been a
colleague of Milligan's in his journalist days and knew
him moderately well. There can't be many of us who
don't have something in our private lives which we
would wish others not to find out; for this to be so
pruriently interesting, and for it to be the only thing the
public will remember, seems to me appallingly sad.**

It was one of those times when you realize why this
government is so uniquely unpopular. By that I do not
mean hated, or detested, but unpopular in a new fashion.
It is, I think, a sense that its members are detached from
life as it is actually lived, unaware of people's concerns,
believing only in a fantasy world where their own dogma
works faultlessly for the national weal.

The question to the prime minister seemed easy
enough. Lynne Jones, the Labour MP for Selly Oak,
pointed out that Mr John Cahill would receive some £10
million when he quits as chairman of British Aerospace.
She asked: 'How can this be justified?'

There are all sorts of simple answers. You can mumble
about regretting such high payments (Mr Major has in the
past) or you could claim that Mr Cahill is worth every
penny if he put more than £10 million on the value of BAe
shares. But he did neither.

'It is not a matter for me,' he said, rather peevishly.
The Labour benches erupted in anger – false anger, to be
sure, but anger which represented their sense of what the
country as a whole might feel about the news. They
shouted and booed and jeered, and someone lowered the
moral tone by adding: 'You pillock!' which is this month's
insult of choice.

Then Angela Eagle, who is becoming an effective
parliamentary operator, rose: 'If you do not believe that a

£10 million pay-off for someone who has just sold our last remaining car industry to foreign competitors is not a matter for you, could you please explain precisely what is a matter for you?'

The prime minister merely asked what forms of intervention or control the Labour Party would propose. Technically, I suppose he is right. BAe could pay Mr Cahill the Gross National Product of Upper Volta every day of the week if it so chose, and it would indeed be none of the government's business. But does he imagine that the electorate as a whole shares his equanimity?

A word about the late Stephen Milligan. He was a former colleague of mine, being Washington correspondent of the *Sunday Times* while I did the same job for the *Observer*. I liked him because he was agreeable, thoughtful, and well informed, so that I read his articles with interest but also some anxiety. He knew an awful lot, and often showed me up.

His private life was a mess: he had an on-off engagement with a beautiful and brilliant English divorcee who was driven to the edge by his total inability to make up his mind. Stephen took the view that he might marry one day, then meet someone he liked even more the next month – a fear that could prevent anyone ever getting married at all.

One year, what with flying to London to discuss his private life, with summits in Moscow, *Sunday Times* staff meetings and internal travel in the US, Stephen acquired enough frequent-flier miles to get two round-the-world tickets, first class. But he was so heartily sick of planes by that time that he drove to the seaside instead.

Then he became an MP, and it was sad to watch the man I had known turn into an ambitious mountaineer on the lower slopes of what passes for power in this country. In private he worked hard for his constituents, and could probably claim the credit for the government's change of mind over British Rail pensions. He represented more BR pensioners than any other MP and appears to have prevented a scheme by which the Treasury would have legally purloined a great deal of their money.

In public, however, he was an obsessive loyalist, always ready with a glutinous question for the prime minister or a burst of ersatz fury against an Opposition which failed to recognize the government's multitudinous accomplishments. Many MPs behave like that, but few are as clever as Milligan and so few cause as much regret. It is not a Faustian deal; their souls are not extorted but somehow go into escrow.

The last thing I wrote about him was rude and of course I now regret that. But he was a politician, and in some respects was lost before he died.

9 February 1994

We were constantly being told that Prime Minister's Question Time would be reformed, and that instead of it being a festival of cheap points-scoring, a sort of ideological car boot sale, it would become a serious and valuable forum for the exchange of information and insights. Not yet.

Prime Minister's Question Time is one of the most hallowed British traditions, dating back into the mists of our island history (as far back as Harold Macmillan, actually). Twice a week MPs, members of the public, and admiring foreign tourists pack into the House of Commons to gaze at the prime minister and ask themselves: 'What exactly is his relationship with Justin Fashanu?'

No, no of course they don't. He has probably never met Justin Fashanu. What they really come to see is the cut and thrust of parliamentary debate, where the Opposition asks the prime minister tough, searching questions, which he ignores.

The members of his own party ask grovelling questions in a combative tone of voice designed to make it appear that they are dragging him to the rack in their fearless quest for the truth.

'Will he agree with me [contemptuous curled lip] that the latest record production figures for [dramatic pause] that fine British invention, the Toilet Duck, [voice begins to rise] prove that the recovery is well underway and that the moaners and whingers opposite [voice rises to a scream so that only dogs and some Liberal MPs can hear it] who love nothing better than selling Britain short ...?' [MP collapses back onto bench, suffering from oxygen starvation, but very happy.]

Yesterday's winner of the Greasy Spoon was Cheryl Gillan (C Chesham). Her question was creepy-crawly enough to begin with, but her manner of asking it made it even more oleaginous, like spraying Dream Topping onto Redi-Whip.

'In his *very* busy day has my right honourable friend had time to see the CBI survey which shows that business confidence in Britain is at an all-time high?'

Labour started growling. 'Orders are up, and the recovery is deepening and widening!' Miss Gillan continued. Labour set up a wall of sound, like Phil Spector, without the Ronettes. It became impossible to hear what Miss Gillan was saying, so conceivably she called Mr Major an 'incompetent pillock'.

Sadly the record shows that she actually said that economic indicators 'boded well'. 'Boding' is something statistics only do in Prime Minister's Questions. Either way, Mr Major had no problem with her query.

11 February 1994

In February, the Back to Basics campaign received
another setback, when Mr Hartley Booth, the MP who
had replaced Mrs Thatcher in Finchley, resigned his
parliamentary private secretaryship after admitting a
relationship with his researcher, a young woman named
Emily Barr. The event (Ms Barr said they had slept
together; Mr Booth denied it) was given added piquancy
by the fact that he was a Methodist lay preacher who had
made great play of family values in his election address.

Mr Ron Thurlow, who is the chairman of Finchley South
Conservative Association and thus an important figure in
Hartley Booth's life, explained a lot at the weekend when
he said 'Back to Basics is dead. The Conservatives should
drop it and get on with ruling the country.'

'Ruling', forsooth! Ruling is what the Queen does in
theory and Mrs Thatcher used to do in practice. What Mr
Major and his ministers do is govern, and not very well.
Take a small example. In 1992 the prime minister made a
crucial speech at the Tory Party conference, a large part
of which was devoted to the subject of motorway toilets
and how we should have more ('U-bend if you want to').
Has a single new motorway toilet been built as a result of
this speech? I doubt it. Even a Stalinist tyrant could by
now have created thousands of motorway toilets in
granite and marble with vast murals depicting, in Mr
Major's case, The Triumph of the Free Market over the
Reactionary Forces of Government Involvement – the
School of Capitalist Realism.

Mr Hartley Booth's real name is Edward, and so he
ought to be known by the more demotic 'Ted'. He is, in
some ways, an interesting chap. Having had the blessing
of Lady Thatcher, he inherited her seat. He then set
about gratifying the present leader of his party by voting
the government line on Maastricht. This riled the
baroness, who was overheard saying: 'Hartley Booth is
stupid, stupid, stupid!'

She summoned Ted to her eyrie in the Lords for a ticking-off. When he refused to change his vote, she is alleged to have declared, with majestic scorn: 'You will be known as a footnote in the history of Finchley!'

The History of Finchley. What a mighty tome that must be! One imagines the chronicle begun by the Monk Aelthred, Abbot of Dollis Hill in 973 AD, as the *Annualia Fincleansis*, now stretching to 27 vast leather-clad volumes, of which 18 alone are dedicated to the Thatcher Years, followed by a single footnote: 'She was succeeded by Ted "Hartley" Booth, of whom little is known.'

15 February 1994

> Environment Questions tend to be dull and my eye was caught by a news item about a man who fed himself to crocodiles in the Ivory Coast because he was upset by the death of the president. Crowds watched for two days as his body was ripped apart in the moat around the presidential palace. 'If President Houphouet is dead, I do not see why I should go on living,' the young man shouted before the crocs started to crunch.

That's the kind of old-fashioned loyalty the Conservative Party used to be famous for, and which it could use some of now. I don't think we'd be hearing too much about a threat to John Major's leadership if one of his most ardent supporters pledged to turn himself into a saurian snack. The question is, who?

I wandered into the House yesterday for Environment Questions and there was the perfect choice: John Selwyn Gummer. He is loyal and true. He is, contrary to received opinion, popular among his colleagues, most of whom would be sorry to lose him. He is certainly bite-sized.

Normally the whips drum up support for the boss by murmuring along these lines: 'Prime Minister most impressed by your contribution ... re-shuffle due any day ... high time your talents were recognized.'

Only fools believe them. If, however, Gummer were to say: 'Vote for John Major, or else I shall become a disgusting mass of shredded flesh, fit only for use in a Benetton ad', that would concentrate their minds a treat.

But will he see where his duty lies? I doubt it. There he was, burbling on about the homeless (he even accused Labour of using the problem of homeless families for 'sordid party political purposes', as if homelessness was, like the death of Stephen Milligan, a tragedy quite unconnected with government policies).

None of this will do. What we want is to see Gummer hanging over a churning pool of ravenous reptiles, nervously awaiting the results of the first leadership ballot.

17 February 1994

The next weekend, the press's frenzy over Back to Basics extended to the Labour Party, when the *News of the World* revealed that Mr Dennis Skinner, the seagreen incorruptible from Bolsover, had been having an affair with his researcher, an American woman. Mr Skinner later said that his own marriage had broken up. 'Middle-aged separated man has relationship with woman slightly younger than himself ' is not much of a story even in these prurient times, but what gave this event its special piquancy was the way Skinner had tried tremendously hard to prevent it from being discovered, turning up at the lady's flat in heavy, but unsuccessful, disguise.

The press and public are allowed into the Commons Chamber only after prayers, about three minutes into the sitting. As we trooped in, all our eyes swerved to one spot: the end of the bench below the gangway on the Opposition side. And there he was. Dennis Skinner was in his accustomed place, majestic as ever on his proletarian throne.

I suppose in a vague way some of us thought he might have bottled out. Or announced his resignation as Beast of Bolsover, in order to avoid creating embarrassment to other beasts, or to spend less time with his family.

But the Casanova of Carlyle Square is made of a huskier fibre. It was essential for him to be there at the start of the day's business. A grand entrance later could have been humiliating. Not because of the Tories; they are rather fond of him. But there can hardly be a Labour MP (or journalist) who has not been read an infuriating lecture on their own moral turpitude by Skinner at one time or another. I have had several. Skinner's problem is that, far from being a revolutionary firebrand, he is deeply smug.

But it was no bowed figure who sat there yesterday. It was a kind of super-Skinner, possibly an animatronic

Robo-Skinner, more convincingly Skinneresque than the real thing.

He folded his arms. He jammed one leg over another (his own, that is). Periodically he glowered up at the Press Gallery. Then he produced an enormous white sweetie, which was presumably a Curiously Strong Mint, but which looked like a horse pill. He somehow got this confection in his mouth and pushed it from cheek to cheek, aggressively.

Alan Duncan, the Tory MP whose inventive house-buying practices led to his own resignation, rose to ask a question. Normally Skinner would have blown him off the benches with a blast of finely tuned sarcasm. Instead he turned to the Labour whip Don Dixon, and shared a joke with him.

Steven Norris was on the government bench for Transport Questions. One hoped that the Bolsover Bonker might have a question for the Eros of Epping Forest, but sadly no. Skinner produced another tennis-ball-sized mint. Then he began to scratch and rub his nose – an important piece of personal grooming, since according to the *News of the World*, it's the only part of him his new neighbours ever see.

The next business was one of the House's periodic discussions of hanging. The late Albert Pierrepoint used to boast that he could have a man dead within 20 seconds of shaking his hand. The Commons takes rather longer, but the ritual is just as closely observed.

There is always a silly speech from a Tory back bencher, in this case Mr John Greenway, who seemed to think it would have been all right to have topped, for example, Mr Winston Silcott – the chap who didn't murder PC Blakelock in the Tottenham riots – because 'opinions differ, but my impression is that the police feel they got the right man'.

(There's a neat modern substitute for the fuddy-duddy

old presumption of innocence. 'Members of the jury, this is a capital crime, but opinions differ, and if on the whole you think the police reckon they have probably got the right bloke, or at least someone who looks a lot like him ...')

At this point, or some equally crass moment, Mr Nicholas Fairbairn intervenes. He points out that he appeared in no fewer than 17 capital cases. 'If I had made a mistake in asking my questions, the man might have gone to' – pause for dramatic silence – 'the trap! Therefore I believe [capital punishment] is evil and wrong in every way, and I have the experience.'

Sadly, Mr Fairbairn has been ill lately and, in his tight black Regency suit (he has always been famous for his bizarre dress sense, often arriving at the House in what can only be called tartan three-piece pyjamas), he made Marley's Ghost look as fit and cheery as Noel Edmunds. He collapsed back into his seat, leading us to hope that some kind shade will soon lead him back to his Unquiet Grave.

I looked across the Chamber for Dennis Skinner, but unfortunately he had gone.

22 February 1994

Later on that same day the House discussed the proposal to reduce the age of consent for homosexuals from 21 to 18 or 16. Edwina Currie, who we last met promoting her lubricious new novel, was the principal speaker and organizer for those who wanted the lowest age.

Edwina lost, but it was a fine, bravura performance. She is not popular anyhow; her colleagues find her brash, self-satisfied and not much better than a pornographer herself. Few will forget the episode in her novel involving the finely balanced strawberry. It's also true that a woman is an easy victim even – perhaps especially – in the House of Commons.

Yet she stood up against a hostile crowd of fellow Tories, and if she didn't change sufficient votes, she had enough guts to shut them up. She began by saying that it was a historic debate. 'Rubbish!' someone shouted, setting the tone for the reception to follow.

She seemed flat and nervous at first. She is not a natural speaker, and her sentences stood separate and prim, like dominoes in a line, rather than flowing into each other. But then the interruptions began.

Each intervention seemed to stoke her fire. Harry Greenway wanted to know what would protect young men from the ravages of older homosexuals. 'As a Tory,' Edwina told him firmly, 'I believe that the state should be kept out of our personal lives. What our neighbours are up to is none of our business.'

Mr Tony Marlow growled: 'Does she want this House to legalize the buggery of adolescent males?'

She smiled sweetly. 'Private sexual behaviour is none of our business – including the honourable gentleman's.' This reference to Marlow, a serial heterosexualist with two large families, brought a laugh from Labour. They were beginning to experience a strange, new disquieting sensation, one which was bound to cause them a painful psychological adjustment: they were beginning to agree with something Edwina said.

She went on: 'The last few weeks [did she mean her own campaign, or the far murkier Back to Basics?] have told me that one person's sexual perversion is another's preferred sexual practice.'

It was no more likely that rapacious middle-aged homosexuals would hang around school gates than rapacious middle-aged straights. 'The idea that young people would be attracted to some middle-aged old piggy ...'

Right on cue, up stood Elizabeth Peacock, to Labour cheers. But by now Edwina was down the home stretch. 'Equality is the only sustainable position. There is no such thing as partial equality. People are equal or they are not.'

She failed [the House voted to lower the age to only 18] but it was a brave failure. We will certainly continue to laugh at Edwina, but we will not quickly sneer again.

22 February 1994

New readers start here: Dennis Skinner, the dashing but caddish Beast of Bolsover, has won the heart of Lois Blasenheim, a sloe-eyed beauty from New York who works as his research assistant by day, and at night makes the Beast with Two Backs with her boss at her apartment in Chelsea's luxurious Carlyle Square.

When Mrs Skinner pines alone in her humble Derbyshire cottage, the rough Beast slouches towards Chelsea in disguise in order to visit Lois. Then, skulking in the shrubbery, not to beat about the bushes, he beats about the bushes.

Now Dennis's and Lois's secret love has been revealed in a sordid rag and exposed to the jeers of an uncaring world. For 48 hours he has maintained a dignified silence, merely tossing the occasional scowl to his tormentors in the Press Gallery, venting his rage and frustration only on a packet of gigantic sweeties – the Mintball as Big as the Ritz.

But yesterday his pride could stand no more. David Evans (C Hatfield) rose to ask a question ostensibly about a community care centre in Lambeth. Mr Skinner lives in Lambeth when he is not in Derbyshire or Carlyle Square.

But Mr Evans is a pretty weak Beast, a jackal compared to Mr Skinner's lion. He pointed at the Opposition benches and demanded: 'Do you think that Lambeth ought to increase their services, since some of that lot over there have taken to being in the bushes in Belgravia during the night?'

It was an utterly meaningless question, but the Tories started cheering. Betty Boothroyd knows very well when MPs are taking advantage of the rules of order – around 95 per cent of the time. 'The question is specific – about Lambeth Community Care Centre – and I do not think they have bushes outside their building,' she said.

But the B-team Beast would not shut up. 'Lambeth needs to have that lot provided with hats and mufflers to keep them warm when they are hiding in these bushes,' Mr Evans persisted, never one to drop a stone until he has tried one last time to extract blood from it.

By this time the Tories were beside themselves with glee, rather like the day Mrs Thatcher resigned. Skinner rose, to cries of 'Where's your muffler?' and football chants of 'Chelsea! Chelsea!' His face went red. His weight shifted from foot to foot, like a boxer preparing to close. He even made a level cutting motion with his hands, as if, with monumental chutzpah, he was ordering the House to silence.

'On the question of community care in Lambeth, or anywhere else, let me say that I am prepared to have my conduct examined at the Despatch Box – if every cabinet minister will have *their* conduct examined.'

Then he began jabbing at the Tory benches with alternate hands – right, left, right. His voice rose from a screaming roar to a Concorde emergency landing. 'Better still, let's have a general election and let the public judge. Then I'll be sat over there, and some of them will be wanting a fresh job!'

The Tory benches erupted in blissful delight. As the health minister Brian Mawhinney feebly responded that Skinner must be glad to have got that off his chest, the familiar northern rumble could be heard: 'This kid's not gonna run away' – still beastly but unbowed.

23 February 1994

In February, the Queen went to Belize and caused a minor controversy there.

The Queen's remarks to the Parliament of Belize the other day have been seen as a coded attack on British government policy. She said that it was never right to tackle crime by looking at the symptoms alone. One had to examine the causes – 'the real roots of the disease'.

A Buckingham Palace spokesman said it was not the case that she had been obliquely criticizing the home secretary, Mr Howard, whose 'lock up the lot' policy has caused some disquiet at home. Instead, the Queen had been following normal constitutional practice, and speaking on the advice given by her Belizean ministers.

Hmm, yes. ('What do you think, Mr Esquivel?' 'I recommend the inculcation of liberal values coupled with a broadened sense of self-esteem, Your Majesty. Alternatively, string 'em up.')

In any case, it was regrettable to see essentially ceremonial figures, such as the present government, being dragged into the mire of party political debate. Mr Major and Mr Howard do a marvellous job for Britain, one which most of us would not do for all the tea in China. If they have political opinions, they are expected to keep them to themselves, and this they manage very well.

Nor are they able to answer back. Admittedly this has more to do with their own hopeless incompetence than any fixed convention. But the fact remains that a constitutional government like ours must never allow itself to get embroiled in the important matters such as crime, the environment and education, which are the rightful preserve of the monarchy.

25 February 1994

I returned from a long weekend in the United States (having foolishly omitted to buy a stack of 'England in World Cup 1994' T-shirts at Boston Airport merely because they cost $35 each) determined to make a close study of Mr William Waldegrave, the minister for open government who, we are told, may be fired from his job so that Mr Major can expiate his guilt to the Scott inquiry into arms sales for Iraq.

Mr Waldegrave is, then, in the unusual position of a turkey being slimmed down for Christmas. However, he seemed poised and relaxed, in no way disconcerted by the vultures overhead. This is perhaps because he is a man of duty, who has no wish to become prime minister – a dangerous figure in any government.

My attention was riveted by something else – Michael Fabricant's hair. Mr Fabricant is the Conservative MP for Mid-Staffordshire and his hair creates something of a metaphysical problem (rather like the old conundrum: is the statement 'this is a lie' itself a lie?). His hair looks so peculiar that everyone assumes that it is a wig. On the other hand, nobody would conceivably buy a wig which looked like that.

It is strawberry blond and has a shiny, plastic sheen. The lower part stands off the face, which implies that it is indeed a syrup (lovable cockney rhyming slang: syrup of figs) yet, from above, it appears to be firmly anchored to the scalp. Overall it looks as if My Little Pony had been in a terrible accident, and its tail had been flung over Mr Fabricant's head.

The owner of the glistening tresses was in an agitated condition. He had a question for Mr Waldegrave. It was clearly a question of great importance. As he awaited his turn, Mr Fabricant tapped his feet nervously. He kept consulting notes scrawled on his order paper. Now and again he looked anxiously at the Speaker, as if afraid that she might forget he was there and skip his question.

Finally he was called. He rose. Was not Megalab (this is some new government wheeze to get children interested in science) a *marvellous* idea? Wasn't it wonderful that the BBC and the newspapers were out and about, promoting it to young people?

He sat down, exhausted. Now and again he stiffened his back, as if to let his body recover from the tension. He crossed and uncrossed his legs, and looked round the Chamber to drink in the triumph of his question.

My guess is that his father Isaac was originally called Oldcastle. He always had an interest in chemistry. One day he invented a wonderful new hair-substitute, possibly a coal-tar by-product. However, the only way it could be fixed was to sew it directly into the scalp. What better way to demonstrate the new textile, now named Miracle Fabricant, than by sewing it on to his son – and changing his name as the ultimate advertising gimmick?

'Nay, Isaac, nay! You cannot do it to your own son!' pleaded Mrs Oldcastle, but in vain. The boy's head was woven. But the new fibre was a terrible disappointment, making only one sale, to Michael Heseltine (whose father, old Jethro Entwhistle, had invented a new brand of hairdressing lotion which he tried out on his son) …

8 March 1994

Like many onlookers, I had begun to suspect that
underneath his blokeish, our man on the terraces in the
rain for the match against Hartlepools' second team
manner, Kenneth Clarke was a fairly calculating fellow.
One of his calculations seemed to be that John Major
might not last for much longer, and that it might just be
possible to speed him on his way out. But I am sure this
is a cynical and unfair judgement.

I have this rather disgusting habit: I shave in the bath. But
I don't apologize, even to my wife, since shaving in the
bath is one of life's most agreeable luxuries. The hot
water soothes the soul, the steam softens the beard, and
the razor glides gently over the face, not so much slicing
the bristles as harvesting them, like young asparagus in
June.

Fortunately my choice of razor (I am not being paid for
this) is the new Wilkinson Protector. This is a curious red
object, streamlined as if it were liable to face powerful
head winds, of a design which might have been called
'space-age' in the fifties. It has a row of tiny filaments
across the twin blades, which prevents them from gouging
your skin or decapitating your carbuncles.

I was glad I was using the Protector yesterday morning
when I heard Kenneth Clarke talking about the future
leadership of the Conservative Party. The chancellor was
at his public bar best. It was, he said, 'one of the folksy
traditions of British politics that you cannot give an
interview about the weather without being asked about
the leadership!' (I wondered idly in the steam whether

Michael Fish has the opposite problem. Invited on the radio to discuss the Tory Party leadership, his interviewer annoyingly keeps asking him whether it's going to rain.)

Mr Clarke added: 'It is a bit daft the flames keep being fanned when it plainly is not a serious issue.'

Then he said firmly: 'John Major will be prime minister to the autumn.' My Protector skittered across the chin and crashed into a now asymmetrical sideburn.

I supposed it was a slip of the tongue, and what he meant was 'to the next election'. On the other hand, 'the autumn' is what many Tory MPs think Mr Major will be prime minister until. Mr Clarke seemed to be suffering from the political version of Tourette's Syndrome, the illness that causes people to say inadvertently what they really think.

However, John Humphreys invited him to take back what he had said, and he declined, averring that he merely meant that after the autumn journalists would stop asking him that sort of question. Every time he was interviewed, he said, the slightest remark about the leadership would be extracted and emblazoned all over the headlines.

Well, of course. If you spend 59 minutes talking about the soaraway British economy and just one minute hinting that one day we'll be rid of that rather dreary chap, that is what is going to happen. As Mr Clarke knows perfectly well.

9 March 1994

Mr William Waldegrave, the minister for the civil service, caused mingled alarm and hilarity in March when he told a committee that ministers frequently misled MPs. 'In exceptional circumstances, it is necessary to say something that is untrue in the House of Commons.' This, he added, was well understood and accepted. He seemed surprised by the fuss his remarks caused. It was widely predicted at the time that this admission would cause Mr Waldegrave to lose his job, though in July the prime minister actually promoted him to agriculture secretary.

The Waldegrave story would be 'dead by teatime', Jeffrey Archer said on the radio yesterday. Normally, if the Labour Party had anything to do with it, it would be dead by elevenses. But for once they got themselves together in time.

Michael Meacher – it is a bold writer who begins a paragraph with those words, but persevere, please. If you get to the end, you may read the ISBN catalogue details, as a treat – Mr Meacher takes the view that while what Mr Waldegrave said may be well known to everyone in Parliament, it nevertheless shocks the public because it reveals a culture of evasion and half-truth.

He is right. I popped in to hear Michael Heseltine yesterday answer Industry Questions, and while nothing he said was a bare-faced lie, it wasn't particularly true, either. A sort of Phil Collins, designer-stubbled lie perhaps.

Someone asked him about David Steel's and John Smith's remarks about the Pergau Dam scandal. Hezza looked scornful. What they said might be important, except that it was 'extremely unlikely that anyone took the blindest bit of notice of either of them.'

In fact, Sir David's speech was widely and approvingly reported. So was Hezza lying? Well … Later, some back bencher asked a drivelling, sycophantic mock-question.

'My honourable friend makes a most valuable point,' said Hezza, a remark which was, at the very least, parsimonious with the truth.

Michael Fabricant asked about inward investment. 'We have made a triumph of inward investment,' Mr Heseltine told him. If he were a wooden puppet, he would not quite resemble Pinocchio, but perhaps Jimmy 'Schnozzle' Durante. As would every other minister.

Nine years ago a civil servant named Richard Mottram famously said during the Clive Ponting case: 'In highly charged political matters, one person's ambiguity may be another person's truth.'

Baron Münchhausen could not have put it better. Why couldn't Mr Waldegrave? After all, the silver-tongued Mr Mottram is now his permanent secretary and sees him every day.

10 March 1994

I recently mentioned the old conundrum: 'Can the statement: "this is a lie" be itself a lie?' It has turned out to be apposite. For example, at Question Time yesterday the prime minister was asked about Mr Waldegrave's thoughts on ministerial tergiversation.

He replied: 'It is not the case now, nor has it been the case in the past, that ministers willingly mislead this House of Commons. That is not the case, and it has not been suggested that that is the case by anyone.'

This is a variant on the classic puzzle, turning an apparently straightforward contradiction into a Möbius strip of paradox. Must the statement 'this is *not* a lie' necessarily *be* a lie if it contains a demonstrable untruth, to wit, that no minister has admitted lying?

It would be nice to cut through all this metaphysical bracken by saying that you can always tell when the prime minister is lying, because his lips move. But that won't do. It's more complicated than that. When he is up against it, eyeball to eyeball with the truth, his speech takes on the weird, distracted, almost surrealistic tinge you can see above.

Or take the first question on the Waldegrave affair yesterday. It came from the Labour MP John McFall. He suggested that the open government minister had given a new meaning to the phrase 'lying in state'.

This is routine parliamentary knockabout, and a passable joke too. Instead, the prime minister looked shocked and affronted, as if Mr McFall had made some gruesomely tasteless remark about, say, poll tax receipts at 25 Cromwell St, Gloucester.

He said grimly that Mr McFall might come, on reflection, to regret the way he had phrased his question. As Labour MPs bellowed 'Why should he?' Mr Major continued: 'If Labour MPs don't regret it, I believe they should.'

Perhaps it was meant to be a threat, in the style of the Kray twins. 'I fink you might regret that, Mr McFall. This a picture of an advance factory in your constituency, is it? Nice looking place, innit? Wouldn't want anyfink to happen to its Gummint orders, now would we?'

Then it got even stranger. Mr Smith asked whether the prime minister realized that what truly undermined the credibility of the administration was the lies they had told about tax during the last election.

Had Churchill risen in the Norway debate in 1940 only to complain about the snoek sandwiches in the Commons cafeteria, the prime minister could not have been more nonplussed.

'I am extremely surprised that you raise that on the day after the IRA's mortar attack on Heathrow Airport, and on the day it has been announced that more troops are to be sent to Bosnia,' he complained.

What a strange cast of mind that revealed. Did he mean that every time the IRA tries and fails to kill someone, all parliamentary debate must be suspended? And how serious does the bad news have to be? 'I am astonished that, in the week when we have learned that *Coronation Street* star Lynne Perrie may be written out of the script, you should raise the question of hospital closures!'

Or, 'It is typical of the party opposite that they should whinge about the unemployment figures on the day after Mr Paul Gascoigne has been involved in yet another tragic fracas in a Rome night club!'

Perhaps it should work the other way round, too. Yet when Lady Olga Maitland pointed out that 'it is Conservative councils which deliver the best services at the lowest possible cost', Mr Major did not angrily denounce her for distracting attention from England's 1-0 defeat of Denmark. No sense of proportion, that man.

11 March 1994

Widening their search outside Parliament, the Sunday papers uncovered an affair between Sir Peter Harding and Lady Bienvenida Buck, who had been the wife of Sir Anthony Buck. Sir Peter was obliged to resign.

In a constitutional theocracy like ours, Almighty God is the nominal head of the Church, though like the Queen, He is advised by His ministers. Or at least, He is advised by Michael Alison, the Conservative MP for Selby and parliamentary spokesman for the Church Commissioners.

So it is always distressing for traditionalists such as

myself to see God being dragged into party politics. He does an absolutely marvellous job which I personally wouldn't want to do for anything. What's more, He is not permitted to answer his critics, unless you count famine, pestilence, plagues of frogs, etc.

Nor can He respond to every wild allegation made by the press. For example, whenever a lightning conductor is ripped off a church tower and plunges like a javelin into the heart of a passing parish priest, like that terrific scene in *The Omen*, it's called an Act of God. But if He denied one unspeakable death, He'd have to deny them all.

God comes the closest to being dragged into British party politics during a rite which takes place once a month in the Commons. MPs are able to ask questions of Mr Alison, whose full title is – pause for roll on the timpani – Second Church Estates Commissioner. The whole session lasts for only five minutes, but for that period the House becomes eerily like a church. The atmosphere is muted; order papers rustle gently like hymn sheets. One expects Mr Tony Newton, the Leader of the House (he looks like a suburban sidesman – you can almost hear him murmuring: 'Bride or groom? Smoking or non-smoking?'), to appear with a cloth bag on a stick for the collection.

This always happens on a Monday when the House is almost empty, so the resemblance to the Church of England is complete. They should take a tip from the evangelicals, and have the clerks play electric organs and tambourines. Now and again Madam Speaker would stand up and sway from side to side, crying 'Praise The Lord!'

But the sense that God should be allowed to stay away from politics does linger, and there was a murmur of disapproval when Tony Banks (Lab Newham NW) asked Mr Alison about the vast losses made by the Church Commissioners through speculation on the property market. He inquired what effect that would have on clergy stipends.

Did this show the Commissioners' incompetence, 'or has Almighty God indicated his strong disapproval of property speculation?'

Mr Alison, the Tory Party's churchwarden, said: 'You will find that clergy's fees are going up rather more than your parliamentary salary this year. Your invocation of the Divinity implies that He is looking on MPs rather less favourably than on the clergy.'

This sounded unfair. Why should He take that view? After all, there are hundreds of pious MPs who have never laid a finger on Bienvenida, Lady Buck (a name invented solely to be the first line of limericks). Yes, scores of MPs! Or at least dozens. And many of them male!

Even more puzzling was the question tabled by Robert Spink. He wanted the courts to name people convicted of sex offences.

'Twenty-one homosexual men were arrested for gross indecency in a public toilet only a few minutes walk from my house,' he said. 'All the public toilets in my constituency have had to be closed at night as a result.'

What was Dr Spink moaning about? Had he hoped to join in the fun? And why did he complain about the closed lavatory being near his home? Why doesn't he use the one there, like the rest of us? (I mean the ones in our houses, not his.)

At this point I might have pointed out how lucky it was that the health minister John Bowis has just launched National Continence Week, with an announcement that 'Continence advisers will be at [this is true] Waterloo Station to hand out helpline stickers to commuters.'

But I am not going to mention illness any more. Dr Jonathan Bindman of the Maudsley Hospital in London takes me to task for misunderstanding Tourette's

Syndrome, from which I accused Mr Waldegrave of suffering.

Looking at his International Classification of Diseases, Dr Bindman suggests that Tory ministers are much more likely to be suffering from 'F60.2, Dissocial Personality Disorder', symptoms of which include 'callous disregard for others, incapacity to experience guilt or to profit from experience ... marked proneness to blame others, or to offer plausible rationalisations'.

15 March 1994

As I just pointed out, the government has declared this National Continence Week. Colourful festivals have been taking place across the land. There are to be balloon races, pelvic-floor exercise workouts, and a conference in London entitled Women and Continence.

I stopped at Waterloo Station yesterday (all of this is entirely true) where the concourse was thronged, or at least dotted, with smartly uniformed 'continence advisers'. They were handing out leaflets under a humorous cartoon poster of a chap who is in such extreme humorous cartoon agonies that he has twisted a bus stop out of shape.

Since it costs 20p to use the toilet at Waterloo (correct change only) this is not quite the place to be reminded of a nagging bladder. Luckily the advisers were also handing out stickers to put on your clothes. These read: 'If you can't always make it to the loo in time, ring 091 213 0050', though if you're in extremis and the pubs are closed, I don't see what help phoning a number in Newcastle is going to be.

Some readers have asked whether National Continence

Week has anything to do with John Major's 'when you gotta go, you gotta go' speech about motorway toilets in 1992. Others wanted to know why I didn't make an amusing joke about cabinet leaks.

The answer is that this column never makes cheap cracks at the expense of people who are suffering from embarrassing medical conditions. If you are about to make a vital presentation to a board of no-nonsense businesspersons and this awful dark stain spread on the front of your trousers, it isn't remotely funny, except to the other people in the room.

Others might claim that I am discussing this topic only to conceal the fact that nothing of interest happened in the Commons yesterday. To them, I say they should remember that the slogan of National Continence Week is 'Don't Suffer in Silence', which is the motto adopted, consciously or not, by all Members of Parliament.

During Prime Minister's Questions, Mr Smith asked Mr Major why in one year the amount that NHS hospital trusts had spent on cars had risen by 65 per cent to some £25 million. 'Do you not realize that most people in this country want money spent on patients and not on cars?' he asked.

The prime minister replied by calling him an 'unreconstructed centralist'. He added, 'More patients are being treated than ever before.'

But everyone I know in the NHS system says that the figures are as easy to massage as Plasticine and mean nothing at all. For example, I wouldn't be a bit surprised to learn that every commuter approached by a continence adviser on Waterloo Station appears somewhere in Mrs Bottomley's magical statistics.

16 March 1994

Prime Minister's Questions is becoming stranger. Not just louder, or more pointless, but more peculiar. People say odd things, for which one cannot always discern a motive or any rational rationale. For example, yesterday Mr Henry Bellingham asked if the Prime Minister was aware that the Labour councils in Birmingham and Manchester had the same debt levels as Paraguay and El Salvador. (Do they teach this kind of crawling at Eton? Is there some esoteric Etonian house or society called Bumsuckers? 'Ooh, sir, what a nice tie, if I may say so, sir! Some more Australian sparkling Brut, sir?')

A normal person would point out that any statistical comparison between a very poor country like El Salvador and a comparatively rich place like Manchester is meaningless. But not MPs.

Mrs Margaret Beckett, the Labour deputy leader, chipped in to point out that Conservative Westminster had a higher debt than Mongolia (except that in Mongolia they presumably don't board up the yurts in the hope that nomadic Tory voters will ride by and take possession).

So – and this is where the exchange took off into the realms of madness, like an old German expressionist film – Mr Major replied that Camden owed more than Chad, and Islington more than Togo. He went on, and on. Bradford, we learned, is deeper in debt than Botswana and Leeds in a bigger financial hole than Lesotho.

(Do they have similar exchanges in Third World parliaments? 'The honourable member may complain that our national debt is now 18 trillion *kwachas*. But since this is only £47.25, it is considerably less than is owed by the profligate Steeple Bumstead parish council!')

What is most depressing is that there are teams of clever and well trained civil servants (and Labour Party researchers) who are paid genuine money to construct these fantasy figures. There is a real debate on the future relationship between council spending and central government. It may occasionally be glimpsed on *Question Time*, or *Newsnight*, but it certainly isn't taking place in the House of Commons.

18 March 1994

> In late March, there was, allegedly, a great dispute in Downing Street between the Prime Minister and the Reverend Ian Paisley. It all sounded a little too convenient to me.

Sir Jimmy Savile is famous for his ebullient personality, but not for his command of the English language. Once, when filming for his programme *Jim'll Fix It* (which should have been re-named 'Jim'll Fix It Provided the BBC Can Get It For Free'), he interviewed a general who had a large collection of Victoria Crosses mounted in an impressive display cabinet.

As the camera panned across, Sir Jimmy waved his cigar and inquired: 'Now, general, is any of these here medals more different from the rest than what the others are?'

It's a good question, which I often ask myself when staring down on the presentation box of Tory MPs called the House of Commons, or at least the right-hand side of it. Are any of them more different to the rest than what the others are?

Sometimes, when they choke with mock indignation about the disloyalty of the Opposition, or grow lyrical about the achievements of the dear leader John Major (it can get uncomfortably like North Korea, with the nuclear bomb, but without the giant statues) one feels, as they sit there with their wire glasses and glossy pates, that they have all been cloned from the same source, perhaps a mosquito which once bit Sir Norman Fowler.

They are the Pod People. This is possibly why some of them go to such lengths to makes themselves more different from the rest than what the others are. Take Mr Nirj Deva, the Tory MP for Brentford, who you might imagine had no need for a distinguishing characteristic, being the only MP of Asian origin on the Tory side (though I have long suspected that Mr Norman Lamont has Burmese blood).

Mr Deva, who asked a Pod Person's question about the environmental impact of British aid, designed to permit the aid minister, Mark Lennox-Boyd, to say that the Pergau Dam would have no harmful effect on the environment, has recently renamed himself Mr Nirj 'Joseph' Deva. Why? Is it to stop us confusing him with all the other Nirj Devas in Parliament?

The other big news yesterday was about the alleged screaming match between Ian 'Kyle' Paisley, and the Rt Hon 'John' Major at Downing Street yesterday. I am generally suspicious when I am told about rows between two people who both have good electoral reasons for falling out with each other. I expect the reality was more like this:

'Marvellous to see you, Ian! I don't suppose I could tempt you to a dry sherry?'

'No, my dear prime minister, the cup that cheers is always stimulation enough for me!'

'Now, Ian, I've had Robin draw up a communiqué about our little tiff. Rather racy, I think you'll agree. If you would care to glance over it …'

'Splendid stuff, John. That should keep the troops in fine fettle! Though in paragraph 7, I'm not altogether sure that I would actually want to bite off your ear!'

'Oh, I don't know, you might very well, you miserable Orange bastard …'

22 March 1994

You might think that the *Food and Drink* programme on BBC2 is scary enough ('coming up next, the menace that lurks in marmalade'). But it is nothing compared to the Commons, which these days is always a Chamber of Terrors. The latest threat is called Temazepam, a sleeping pill which, unaccountably, some people inject in gel form.

How does anyone learn about such things? Who is so utterly desperate that they say: 'Ooh, a sleeping pill. I think I'll take that out of its plastic capsule and shove it up my arm,' when they could get a similar effect from two cans of Special Brew?

Anyhow, MPs worked themselves into a froth of agitation about Temazepam. Just when Joyce Quin was talking about people who commit crimes under its influence, in, with perfect timing, walked John Major.

One of the first Tories up was Mr Gyles Brandreth, the Tory MP for Chester, who lost some £200,000 of our money on a ghastly Royal Heritage museum in the Barbican. Naturally it was a failure. With the current standing of the Royals, I doubt whether anything short of Princess Di's Wonderbra would bring in the punters.

(What made Mr Brandreth's arrangement especially piquant was the fact that the money came from the Treasury, where he is a parliamentary private secretary. Nothing wrong with that, of course. However, as the American commentator Michael Kinsley once said, the scandal isn't what's illegal, but what's legal.)

Mr Brandreth offered an excuse at the time. He said that it was important for MPs to have experience of business, and that meant experience of business failure as well as success. Whether the taxpayer would regard £200,000 as money well spent for Mr Brandreth's on-the-job training is another matter. And why do Conservative MPs always feel that it's experience of business they should acquire? Why do none of them ever become a supply teacher or a hospital porter?)

'Siddown!' 'Pay it back!' and other endearments came from the hooligans opposite.

Mr Brandreth is definitely oily. He is, as the old ad said, liquid engineering. I once appeared on an obscure radio programme with him and Ms Katie Boyle who was, she told us, about to take part in a charity motor race.

'Oh, Katie,' said Mr Brandreth, gazing into her eyes, 'on Sunday, all our thoughts will be with you.'

I wanted to say: 'Mine won't. I'll have forgotten about it the moment I walk out.' Being a coward, I didn't.

Mr Brandreth would have gazed into the prime minister's eyes too; luckily the Chamber is not configured like that. But, he cooed, would Mr Major agree with him about the 'uniquely beautiful city of Chester' (his constituency) which, like the rest of Britain, was now roaring out of recession? Mr Major had little trouble dealing with that poser.

Next John Smith asked whether it was right for the well-to-do to avoid VAT by paying their fuel bills in advance, while the poor would have to pay in full later. Mr Major said there was 'nothing unusual' in the arrangement, as if sending £7,500 to Norweb was much the same as getting in a crate of beer before the Budget.

Then suddenly the Temazepam kicked in. 'You are up to your old tricks!' he shouted at Smith. 'Telling people how to spend their money! You are a meddler in everything ...'

Next, Mr Giles Radice asked one of the new slimmed-down compact questions which sometimes do bother Mr Major. Was a 23-vote blocking majority more important than enlargement of the European Union? A tricky one that, since Mr Major has staked a lot of British prestige on both.

At that the prime minister was off and running. Temazepam Man's rage against Belgium and Holland, for holding out against him over the blocking mechanism, was as nothing to his fury at John Smith.

'The right honourable gentleman likes to say "yes" to everything that comes out of Europe!' he read from a piece of paper. 'He is "Monsieur Oui", the poodle of Brussels!'

Isn't it weird? Any moment now I expect to hear a high-pitched bleeping as the Mother Ship returns for Mr Major.

23 March 1994

Nicholas Soames is the minister for food and a walking advertisement for his department. Yesterday afternoon he was at the Despatch Box (possibly filled with a few nourishing treats to guard against Question Time starvation). He told bemused MPs that he had probably eaten more Tesco sandwiches than most of them.

I knew Tesco was trying to go upmarket, but this is preposterous. Do they really make clingfilm-wrapped lobster and caviar sandwiches? Or pâté de foie gras and Kraft cheese squares in a wholemeal seeded bun? But then why not? Now that Dudley Moore has discredited himself by beating up his girlfriend, Mr Soames would be a perfect replacement. I see him in morning dress, comically searching for truffles in an Italian forest.

Next Harry Greenway asked about the export of horses for eating. 'If they must devour horses,' he said, referring to the filthy Europeans who are no doubt even now trying to force Douglas Hurd to eat the roast horse of Olde Englande, 'will he promise that, like me, he will never eat a horse as long as he lives?'

MPs waited in suspense. How many times had they heard the minister announce that he *could* eat a horse? None could ever recall him saying: 'Blimey, I could murder a Tesco low-cal egg mayonnaise sandwich!'

He was majestic in reply. 'The House should know,' he announced slowly and solemnly, as if declaring war, 'that I have never and will *never* eat a horse!' It was a heart-warming speech and, coming from anyone except a member of the present government, one might have taken it without a pinch of salt. Or mustard.

The next question concerned the sad story of New Forest ponies, who used to be sold as gourmet snacks on the Continent, but since a fall in prices, now go for medical experimentation in Glasgow.

Now, suppose Mr Soames were to be offered a delicious *filet mignon de cheval de la Forêt Nouvelle* in a *mousseline* of Roquefort, basil and pinenuts, with a decent bottle of Le Richebourg to wash it down? After all, we know from Mr Waldegrave that it is all right for ministers to fib in certain circumstances and Mr Soames, being hungry, would certainly qualify for that.

25 March 1994

Towards the end of March, Mr Major went to an EU
summit meeting in Greece, where he failed to persuade
the other nations to support him on the question of the
size of the blocking majority for EU decisions. The
details are much too dreary to recount, but the prime
minister had made much of his determination to win this
particular fight. Douglas Hurd, the foreign secretary,
had appeared at a Tory conference in Plymouth just
before flying to the summit looking deeply depressed,
dejectedly tossing his car keys into the air as he briefed
the press. He was obliged to return to Westminster on
the Monday to explain, as best he could, the
government's position.

The foreign secretary rose to a complete and eerie silence
from his own benches, but that didn't matter. The body
language told us all we needed to know. Few of the Tories
seemed to have any idea what to do with their hands:
some had them jammed under their chins, others tucked
behind their backs; some kept them folded daintily on
their laps.

Mr Lilley was one of those, and then suddenly leaned
right back, as if being garrotted by a passing commando.
Mr Gummer was both hunched and twisted round at the
same time, like a penitent trying to squeeze into a
confessional for pygmies. Mr Clarke wrapped his arms
right round himself, as if he was inside an invisible
straitjacket. And they all looked utterly miserable.

All, that is, except Douglas Hurd. He seemed relaxed
and cheerful, especially compared to the despondent
figure who flew off to Greece last Friday. Then he had
looked as if invited to a Tupperware party at the House of
Atreus. Something in the past twenty-four hours had
caused him to be comprehensively regruntled. Perhaps he
is going to resign.

More likely his élan had something to do with the fact
that he was going to face Dr Jack Cunningham who is,

mysteriously, Labour's spokesman on foreign affairs. Dr Cunningham's ability to misread the House of Commons is unparalleled. Stevie Wonder would have less trouble with a newspaper. As Mr Hurd said, 'An occasion which might have been rather difficult has become rather a pleasure, thanks to you.'

At a time like this, all the Labour spokesman has to do is to watch the Tories swing gently in the wind, creaking like the lynch victim at the start of an Italian western. A couple of deceptively mild yet probing questions, or perhaps a laconic Clint Eastwood remark pushed past the cheroot: 'You done a bad thing, boy.' But Dr Cunningham decided to do all he could to get unhappy back benchers behind Mr Hurd. 'The House has rarely heard such a squalid and dubious statement from him ...'

Mr Hurd relaxed. Behind him the massed Brigade of Brown Nosers got to work. (Did they all win merit badges in the scouts, a grease stain worn proudly on the sleeve, perhaps?) Mr Tim Renton actually congratulated him on the agreement, a humiliating defeat for the British government which Mr Renton chose to term a 'compromise'.

'Oh, I think congratulations are a shade premature,' Mr Hurd said, accurately.

Mr Bowen Wells rose to praise his 'typical honesty, courage and responsibility in the negotiations'. The foreign secretary said that he was grateful for these epithets, 'but I do find that one lurches from excessive praise to excessive criticism, and I am in the middle of one such lurch at present.'

While attending the Conservative Central Council meeting in Plymouth, I was lucky enough to obtain a book titled *MPs in Verse*, written by a colleague in the press gallery called Nikki van der Zyl.

She uses poetry to draw portraits of several MPs, including Mr Hurd:

His stiffness and aloofness send,
Respect and awe across the sea,
He does his job devotedly,
A decent foreign secretary.

29 March 1994

> The following day the prime minister had the unpleasant
> experience of coming to the House of Commons to
> explain the débâcle of Greece. It was more embarrassing
> for him than for Mr Hurd, who had managed to signal
> that he himself had not been in favour of the carry-on at
> all. The exchanges included the first public call from a
> Tory MP for Mr Major to resign.

By a happy coincidence, this year marks the bicentenary of
the unsuccessful Flanders campaign against the French led
by Frederick Augustus, Duke of York (no direct relation
to the hoydenish figure who holds that title now). It is this
setback which is commemorated in the nursery rhyme.

So it was apt that the Grand Old Duke's modern suc-
cessor should have to make a statement to the Commons
explaining similarly unsatisfactory events on the Continent. The prime minister told MPs that it was absurd to
suggest that his decision to march his men back down the
hill was, in any meaningful sense, a 'climbdown'.

Opposition MPs pressed him to say why he had led
them up the hill in the first place, when it should have
been quite clear that there was no escape route other than
in a downward direction.

One's mind drifted gently back 200 years. Beau
Skinner, an elegant figure in a powdered wig (pulled
down over his nose) called it a 'bleeding humiliation',
caused by 'a pathetic attempt to suck up to all them

Hanoverian factions – including that lot over there who are after your dukedom.'

The duke replied that the ascent had been 'a highly valuable exercise, bringing real benefits to the British people, benefits the Whigs would have thrown away by never attempting the climb in the first place.

'Those who argue that when we were up we were up, and when we were down we were down, betray once again their complete ignorance of modern warfare.

'We were not inconsiderably both at the same time, an achievement of which the whole country can be proud.' Replying to charges that his men had been driven out of Flanders after an incompetent and bungled campaign the duke said, amid cries of 'Worrabout Bunker Hill, you great pillock', that it was 'arrant nonsense. The so-called retreat was an interim re-grouping measure, which will be resolved in further talks with our French colleagues.'

I snapped unwillingly back to 1994. An improbable figure, also apparently wearing a powdered wig, was still haranguing the prime minister. Mr Tony Marlow – ah yes, it was just his white hair which misled me – was yelling at him. 'As of now you have no authority, credibility or identifiable policy ... Why don't you stand aside and make way for somebody else who can provide the party and the country with direction and leadership?'

Given the scale of this most recent *bouleversement*, Mr Major was fortunate to have Mr Marlow as his most public opponent. He may see himself as heir to Leo Amery, or even Cromwell, but sadly none of his colleagues do.

(I learn that the original Duke of York continued as commander-in-chief for many years, surviving a bribery scandal involving his mistress, and several more military disasters. So there is hope for John Major yet.)

30 March 1994

> In Italy, Signor Berlusconi became prime minister. It
> soon became clear that our own government was happy
> to overlook the presence of neo-fascists in his cabinet,
> since our ministers were desperate for allies in the
> European Union.

Yesterday the eyes of Europe turned on the astonishing
new political force which, by forging an ad hoc right-wing
coalition, plans to sweep away years of government
incompetence in a country where scandal and corruption
are woven into the very fabric of politics.

Unfortunately *Hezza Britannia* wasn't around. The
House of Commons operates in such a mysterious way
that the man of the moment never seems to be there –
though he had made a dignified statement to the nation in
the morning at that more senior forum, the *Today*
programme.

The problem for Mr Heseltine is that he isn't really a
retail politician. Rousing speeches to mass rallies – fine.
Intimate chats with potential supporters – trickier. He's
not great at the one-on-one, far better at the one-on-ten
thousand.

Essentially he is a loner. He isn't to be found hanging
round the bar hoping to buy someone a drink. He seems
to have learned how to solicit support from a
correspondence course.

> *Hezza*: Hello! Yes, er, I gather you wanted to have a
> word with me about interim grants for business
> start-ups in development areas such as your own.
> *Tory MP:* No.
> *Hezza:* Well, jolly good. If I can be of any further
> help, please don't hesitate to get in touch.

I recently quoted the words of Nikki van der Zyl,
whose slim volume has made her widely loved as the
McGonagall of the Lobbies. In a far-sighted poem called

'Michael Heseltine', written five years ago, she said:

> You've got the bluest eyes I ever seen,
> You're tall, good looking and you're
>   lean.
> Some think that you will Leader be
> When Maggie goes – well, we will see!
> You work so hard around the land,
> Speaking to the faithful band.
> But as you know, life's full of spills,
> And Fate not always Hope fulfils.

The last line has, I feel, a genuine ring to it, and I hope Mr Heseltine pays heed.

31 March 1994

After the Easter break, MPs returned invigorated for a row about whether two patients had been turned away from NHS hospitals because they were thought to be too old to be worth treating.

Prime Minister's Question Time has gone beyond awfulness these days. It isn't even amusingly kitsch any more. It resembles, perhaps, some terrible local radio station where the studio manager has fallen into a drunken stupor.

The wrong tapes are played, at the wrong speed. Meaningless remarks are followed by storms of unintelligible noise; maniacs are allowed on air and blather dementedly while the presenter is out getting drunk.

Yesterday began in reasonably humdrum fashion. Mrs Beckett asked the prime minister about the two septuagenarians who were apparently refused treatment because of their age. (Mr Smith is at home, nursing his ligaments after a climbing accident. Being 55, he is ten years short of the cut-off point and still qualifies for medical treatment.)

In at least one of the cases there seems to have been a genuine mistake, and the facts remain unclear. Which meant of course that each side in the Commons took up fixed and ferocious positions.

Mr Major accused Mrs Beckett of scaremongering (for some reason she is better at needling him than Mr Smith is; maybe it's her Violet Elizabeth Bott smile which drives him round the twist. Mr Kinnock used to complain that some deep-seated, inbred notion of politesse prevented him from being as rude to Mrs Thatcher as he should, because she was a woman. Possibly Mr Major has the same problem with Mrs Beckett.)

She said that these days doctors faced this kind of unpleasant predicament all the time.

The prime minister, as so often when the truth lies on neither side but is stranded, gasping, in no-man's-land, looked shocked. 'Despite the fact that you have peddled an untruth, you continue to do so again!'

(I always enjoy his quaint metaphors. This one raised an image of Mrs Beckett with a scarf wound round her head, standing at a bus shelter with a basket, crying: 'Buy my lucky untruths, dearie!')

However, peddling untruths is thought to be unparliamentary language, and a great mock hubbub ensued. Betty Boothroyd joined in, saying calmly that she was sure the prime minister would reflect on what he had said, and withdraw the remark. The hubbub increased. 'Order!' shouted the Speaker. A handful of MPs sat down. Mr Major rose to answer the next question.

'Sit down!' the Speaker ordered.

It was a fine stand-off between the two most important

people in the building and solved in a typically ingenious fashion. He didn't withdraw, but he did rephrase his remark, and Ms Boothroyd decided that was good enough for her.

Then Mr David Evans, the human bullhorn who sits for Welwyn, raised the topic of his wife Janice. Mr Evans is trying (and failing) to turn Janice into a much-loved national figure, a heart-warming embodiment of plain common sense. No doubt he hopes she will get her own TV show (*Ooda Thought It!* with Janice Evans), endorsements, souvenir duvet covers and so on. This time he tried in the manner of a market trader.

Janice wished to know, was it the Conservatives who had imposed a top rate of income tax at 40 per cent? 'No-o-o,' bellowed the Tories, even though that's exactly what the top rate is at present. '60? 70? 90? Niney-ay [98],' he yelled, in a reference to the old high supertax rate under Labour, which in retrospect does seem rather a lot. I am glad that Janice is wealthy enough to feel threatened by the possibility of its return.

Anyhow, the whole event was barking. In a properly run radio station, they would have a tape delay, to cut off the loonies.

(This does not always work. In the early days of London broadcasting, one of its parliamentary reporters told me about a disaster that had occurred during a late-night phone-in on the subject of leisure. A woman with a dreary, monotonous voice had rung in, boring the presenter into thinking about something else entirely. So when she said: 'I don't know why people are always complaining that they haven't got enough to do. I mean, you can read good books, or go for long walks in the countryside, or suck men's ...' the offensive words had been broadcast before the poor chap realized what was happening. The Commons often creates the same startling, if less prurient, effect.)

15 April 1994

I have worries about Ann Clwyd, the Labour MP for Cynon Valley. She used to write for the *Guardian*, which is suspicious enough.

Then there's the matter of the name. Originally it was Lewis. Now she is named after a Welsh administrative region. Nobody ever married an administrative region, so there must be another explanation.

A Welsh colleague tells me that Clwyd is actually a 'bardic name', whatever that is. Her bitchier colleagues suggest that she changed it in order to get a Welsh seat. It's as if I, also a *Guardian* writer, were to change my name to Simon Humberside.

Last week she spent 27 hours underground, sitting-in at the last deep coal pit in Wales, and returned to the surface, face fetchingly smeared with coal dust, only when British Coal agreed to postpone the closure. Four days later, the pit shut down anyway.

So yesterday Ms Denbighshire and Flint (as she was known before local government reorganization) accused British Coal and the employment secretary David Hunt of 'lying through their teeth'.

Naturally she was rebuked by the Speaker. Members of Parliament constantly get away with telling fibs. They even, *vide* Mr Waldegrave, get away with admitting that they get away with telling fibs. What's not allowed is for one MP to accuse another of telling the fibs in the first place.

On being rebuked (another colleague tells me that she

was also known as Ann Roberts at one time. How very
unlike the home life of our own dear Queen, who has just
as many names but keeps them simultaneously), she
changed this to 'telling blatant untruths'. Finally she
switched it to 'peddling untruths', which is the phrase
John Major just got away with a week ago.

Ms Boothroyd became genuinely angry. You can
always tell. She starts out with a genteel accent, rather
like Annie Walker in *Coronation Street*. As her gorge
rises, the northern accent becomes steadily more
pronounced and you expect her to roar that she is about
to put the towel back over the taps.

One Labour woman told me afterwards that the whole
row was about Ms Clwyd's desire to get back into the
Shadow Cabinet in the autumn. But I could not agree
with such a catty judgement.

Later the House agreed to give a first reading to a bill
which gave equal treatment to women in the provision of
public lavatories. Naturally there were lots of cheap
jokes. It was the House of Commons at its best, tackling
an issue which it can actually do something about.

Unlike the situation in Bosnia, which also exercised the
House this week. There's nothing they can do there, so
they talk about it at ponderous length. One Labour MP,
Dale Campbell-Savours, actually said: 'If Margaret
Thatcher had been prime minister, she'd have sorted out
this bloody nonsense years ago.'

It's the kind of line you might get from a right-wing
Tory MP after his third Scotch, said offensively loud so
that soggier colleagues can hear it. Or a taxi driver. (Do
MPs also boast about the celebrity cab drivers they've
met? ' 'Ere, I had that Fred Housego in the front of my
cab once.')

20 April 1994

In April, Actors' Equity protested against the number of
politicians who were being used on TV shows. And there
were a lot. It was a rare daytime quiz which didn't
feature the Kinnocks – at least before their elevation to
serious jobs in Europe. On the Tory side, Jerry Hayes
was seldom off our screens. Austin Mitchell and Norman
Tebbit had their own weekly slanging match on Sky TV.
The knack seems to be for the politician to obtain a
distinct personality, like a character in a soap opera.
Cantankerous is good, so is ingratiating. Rhodes
Boyson, for example, does a brisk trade in the whiskery
old geezer whose robust common sense hides a heart of
gold. Charles Kennedy is the saucy young fellow-me-
lad. Being yourself is never quite enough.

What a whingeing lot actors can be! Now they want to ban
politicians from appearing in TV sitcoms, quiz shows and
adverts. (Would this also apply to the tub of lard which
deputized for Roy Hattersley on *Have I Got News For
You?*)

I can understand the thespians' annoyance, but the
problem springs from the fact that there are far more
people who want to be actors than there is work for them
to do. They are in a buyers' market.

So are politicians. They too have a hundred rivals
chasing every job. They are subject to the mad vagaries of
public opinion. They likewise cling to the view that all
publicity is good publicity, and I can think of few
showbusiness people who couldn't learn valuable lessons
here from Edwina Currie, who perhaps is even now
appearing on a five-hour radio phone-in on the Isle of
Mull, and would be doing the same even if she weren't
engaged in a difficult battle to hold the Milton Keynes
seat in the European Parliament.

Actors also play a valuable role in modern British
politics. For instance, they read out the words of the Sinn
Fein leader Gerry Adams, whose own voice is thought by
our leaders to be so commanding and hypnotic that voters

must not hear it, lest we are mesmerized into supporting the IRA. What do they imagine would happen if we could hear Mr Adams as well as see him? 'Funny, yesterday I thought blowing up small children for political purposes was, well you know, wrong. Now for some reason today I think it's fully justified. Can't work it out ...'

There are, quite literally, ads in *The Stage* newspaper on these lines: 'Fingal O'Flahertie. Irish character parts (Gerry Adams a speciality).' Often the actors sound perfectly decent and reasonable people, whereas Mr Adams's real voice is rather dull and rasping. But if it works for him, why not for others? Mr Major's voice could be played by Michael Crawford in his *Some Mothers Do 'Ave 'Em* style; the vocal timbre is almost identical. Mr Smith should be played by the late Andrew Cruikshank, gruff and reassuring.

Mr Portillo could be read by Andrew Sachs, who played the Spanish waiter Manuel in *Fawlty Towers*.

> *Tory MP:* Will the chief secretary agree with me that all the economic indicators bode well for a bright, prosperous future in this country under the courageous leadership of him and his other right honourable friends?'
>
> *Mr Portillo: Qué?*

If actors persist in their demands, I suggest that MPs could fight back by banning actors and TV personalities from politics. We would lose Glenda Jackson and Austin Mitchell, which we might regret, but we would also lose Gyles Brandreth, whose personal drain on the public purse (£200,000) could keep two dozen single-parent families for a year.

Another victim would be Andrew Faulds, who used to play Jet Morgan and Carver Doone, and whose 30th anniversary in Parliament is now upon us. Yesterday he stood up with his magnificent beard akimbo (when it needs a trim, he doesn't go to a barber, but a topiarist). Betty Boothroyd had just complained that members were saying too much and were slowing Question Time down.

Mr Faulds boomed that it would help if 'we could revert to the old custom by which nobody bothers to thank you for allowing them to ask a question.

'Many of the new calibre of MPs try to curry favour with you by saying "thank you", when you are merely doing your job.'

Ms Boothroyd looked mildly peeved. 'I wish all members were as courteous to each other as you seem to think they are. I welcome a "thank you", now and again,' she said, rather coyly, as if Mr Faulds had criticized the kind of young man who sucks up to girls by giving them flowers and chocolates.

To be fair, both sides were wrong. Most MPs know all about serious brown-nosing and it rarely stops at 'thank you'. 'Your wise judgement and far-famed sagacity are once again in evidence, Madam Speaker ...' would be a mere opener for some of these boys. In fact, 'thank you' is little more than a form of throat-clearing, a problem which has never faced Mr Faulds in his whole life.

21 April 1994

'Never trust anyone called Simon,' has always been an important personal motto for me. It's a sound, if not invariable rule, which I commend to you.

Most Simons turn out to be disc jockeys, crimpers or riff-raff of one kind or another. Mr Simon Burns, a Tory back bencher, is terrifically creepy. Even Simon de Montfort, sometimes regarded as the founder of our legislature

– the father of the mother of parliaments, so to speak –
was a frightful anti-Semite, though to be fair anti-
Semitism was the political correctness of the 13th century.

They probably held pro-prejudice workshops, and wore
admonitory badges on their tabards saying, 'Are You a
Racist? You'd Be So Much Nicer If You Were.'

Yesterday however Mr Simon Hughes, the LibDem
MP, asked quite a good question. He wanted to know
how it was that, although Uganda is one of the five
poorest nations on earth, it still has to give back £200
million to the IMF, which is one of the richest
organizations in the world.

'How can that be justified?' he asked. 'And, if not,
what can we do about it?'

The voice of Dame Elaine Kellett-Bowman – it makes
Harrison Birtwhistle sound like Mantovani's Silken
Strings – sliced through the air like a ninja blade.

'Take 'em over again!' she shrilled.

That's what I envy about some MPs: their utter certainty, coupled with their nostalgic yearning for a simpler
past. We can't even take over the Bosnian town of Gor-
azde, and here's a back-bench Tory fondly recalling an age
when we could occupy a whole country with the stroke of a
pen and two companies of illiterate infantrymen.

Kim Howells, from Labour's front bench, asked the
foreign secretary why we weren't sending troops to
Rwanda. 'Is there one law for Europeans and another for
black Africans?' he asked scornfully.

Why, yes. Hadn't anyone told him? Rwandans are
thousands of miles away. Nobody you know has ever
been on holiday in Rwanda. And Rwandans don't look
like us. They have even less clout than Bosnian Muslims.

Of course Mr Hurd couldn't admit that. Instead he said
that the UN hadn't mandated the troops in Rwanda to do
anything useful. 'There is no magic in keeping troops
there if there is nothing for them to do.'

Help came – or appeared to come – from an unexpected quarter. Dennis Skinner, the Beast of Belgravia, rose to make a useful point. The problem had been made worse by the Gulf War, he said, which had encouraged people to think that the same results could be achieved anywhere. In fact, the Bosnia situation was much closer to Vietnam than to the Gulf.

He continued. 'If we sent troops proportionately to the 27 civil wars going on all over the world ...'

Mr Hurd looked as pleased as Mr Hurd ever looks but dubious as well. When you get a gift horse from Dennis Skinner, you don't just look it in the mouth, you give it a blood test and ram it through an airport security scanner, just to be on the safe side.

'... everyone up to the age of 40 – *including Portillo!* – would have to be in uniform. And the royal family would have to do a bit of fighting as well.'

The foreign secretary sounded weary, even a little crumpled. 'You started excellently, and then spoiled it totally by the end,' he told Skinner.

How true about almost everything the present government does, except they seem to start off badly as well. But we cannot really blame them for Bosnia. The spectre of impotence is the most terrifying shade of all.

26 April 1994

Richard Nixon died in April.

The phrase of the moment at Westminster is 'the quiet majority'. It was coined by Mr Portillo last Friday, round about the time that the inventor of the term 'silent majority', Richard Nixon, was joining the Choir Invisible, if they'll have him.

The press, both here and in the United States, has been far too kind to Nixon. From his earliest days in politics he was a deceitful, twisting, amoral crook who would tell any lie to advance his career, even if it meant that innocent people went to jail. Those who point out that our own government was prepared to do the same in the Matrix-Churchill case underestimate the depths of Nixon's vile cynicism.

Naturally when MPs discuss the quiet majority, they do it at the top of their voices. Mr Smith asked the prime minister about the revelation – in a report by the Cabinet Office efficiency unit – that some £500 million had been spent by the government on outside consultancies, with a mere £10 million savings being effected as a result.

'Does the Prime Minister not realize that families throughout Britain, the real quiet majority, facing huge tax increases, will bitterly resent this further example of the government's now legendary incompetence?' Mr Smith inquired.

('Legendary incompetence' has a nice ring to it. One vaguely imagines old men telling yarns of how Sir Major rode out to do battle with the Greene Knighte, but got his lance caught up in his gaskins.)

Sir Major implied that the consultancies were not actually meant to save money but to do jobs, such as designing weapons systems, which civil servants can't manage. In fact, this government is hypnotized by consultants. Their reasoning seems to be that civil servants work for less money than they could earn, and are therefore idiots, to be disregarded. Consultants, however, are paid enormous sums and therefore must be clever. If we pay them even more money, they'll become even more clever.

Mr Smith asked whether the Tories' 'game' was to delay the bad news until after the local and European elections. 'Why not tell the truth before an election?'

The Conservatives decided that this amounted to a charge of lying. They raised the roof with ersatz anger. Betty Boothroyd asked Mr Smith to clarify matters by repeating the remark, which he did with lip-smacking relish. The Tories booed even louder. It became impossible to hear anything at all.

Moments later, Jonathan Evans said that the 'real quiet majority' in his constituency heartily agreed with the government over New Age travellers. I hope that the quiet majority doesn't now appear in every debate. They'd never get a word in edgeways.

The other highspot of Question Time was the appearance of Sir George Gardiner, who has let it be known privately that he might just possibly be persuaded to run against the prime minister in a leadership election this autumn. 'Stalking horse', shouted the Opposition. Actually, Sir George looks more like a stalking ghost – or rather, the character Plug in the Bash Street Kids who, we were told the other day, is to be redrawn because he makes an undesirable role model for ugly children.

The main business of the day was the Police and Magistrates' Courts Bill, whose bleeding and battered body has somehow dragged itself from the House of Lords, where it had been waylaid by anarchic ruffians such as Willie Whitelaw and the Lord Chief Justice.

I decided to take a keen interest in the crucial issues addressed by the bill, but was distracted by the many neologisms created by the home secretary's extraordinary accent. Yesterday we gained 'Chiff Conn-stibble' and a class of officers known as 'middill minigemint'. I do hope Mr Howard is reshuffled. Then we can enjoy what he does to the language in a new field of endeavour: Igriculture, perhaps, or Transpitt.

27 April 1994

An astonishing written answer in the Lords this week revealed that until November last year, businessmen – mostly in Northern Ireland, I imagine – could claim tax relief for the money they paid to extortionists and blackmailers.

Since the IRA and the Protestant para-militaries rely on these shakedowns for much of their income, it must be quite a blow to have the loophole closed. Now, after 25 years, our vigilant ministers have decided that the British taxpayer need no longer help pay for the arms and ammunition needed to kill British soldiers and civilians.

I don't want to labour the point, but it does seem to me to prove again what has been true for a long time now: the Northern Ireland troubles have become institutionalized. There's no real pressure to end them. If even the protection rackets are tax deductible, why should anyone want a solution?

There were several reminders of this during Northern Ireland Questions yesterday. For example, the junior minister Sir John Wheeler said that the subvention to Northern Ireland from the British Exchequer, excluding security costs, came to £3,983 million. This works out at more than £6,000 for every household in the province.

Six thousand smackers in every home! Of course it doesn't come in the form of used notes. It's unemployment pay, or money for new roads or some such. But that's still an awful lot of cash sloshing round in a small economy.

Then someone asked how many people had died so far this year as a result of terrorism. 'This year, I regret to say,' Sir Patrick Mayhew intoned with what is generally regarded as the fitting air of dolour, 'that 19 deaths have been caused by terrorist action.'

Well, apart from the suffering caused to those individuals and their families, that is wonderful news and a cause for rejoicing. We are on target for fewer than 60 deaths in a year, which would be a record low since the Troubles began. Ulster is now a much safer place than, say, Omaha, Nebraska, usually seen as the quintessentially quiet mid-western city.

(The other day the Committee of Public Accounts investigated the appalling number of deaths on Northern Ireland roads, and learned that well over twice as many people are killed by cars as by terrorism. For uninvolved civilians, the ratio is nearer to 15 to 1. But nobody seems to care much about the anguish and suffering caused to those victims. In Northern Ireland, the only thing that counts is how you die.)

No wonder the Unionists and the IRA have been dancing around the Downing Street Declaration, inspecting it, prodding it, and doing everything except agree to it. The fact is that, for them, peace has become much too risky, would cost too much, and would upset far too many people.

(At the end of August the IRA did announce a cease fire. But no one knew if this meant a genuine end to the Troubles or was merely – as Gerry Adams claimed – another stage in the 'struggle'.)

29 April 1994

By early May, it seemed that Mr Major's tenure in Downing Street must be almost at an end. Tory MPs – admittedly the eccentrics, the loonies and riff-raff for the most part – were calling for him to go. The humiliating débâcle over European Union voting was still fresh in people's minds. Mr Michael Heseltine was on form and his acolytes and satraps were touring the corridors and bars assuring MPs that his heart attack had been caused by a minor blockage, not by any weakness in the heart itself. The only question in some minds was who would act as the 'stalking horse', a candidate who had no hope of being elected but who would allow MPs to register their dissatisfaction with Major.

Labour MP Brian Donohoe asked the prime minister yesterday to glance round his own front bench and tell the House 'who he thinks his Brutus will be'.

Mr Major: I think you have mistaken the time of year – we are past March!'

Laugh? We almost started. But a lot of Conservatives chortled away for – oh, whole seconds, with all the loyal merriment of a studio audience.

The error is to view Mr Major's possible demise as a dramatic tragedy. It's much closer to a situation comedy, full of wacky characters and smart-alcc punchlines.

This is why, when the prime minister speaks, Tory MPs feel obliged to provide a laugh track which seems to have been spliced on to the tape after a studio recording.

For instance, John Smith asked whether he thought it wasn't extraordinary that a senior member of the 1922 Committee (believed to be David Evans MP, who is a senior member of the 1922 Executive in the sense that Jeremy Irons is a senior actor – he may be senior all right, but that doesn't make him any bloody good) should have called for the resignation of the Tory chairman and the local government minister, the Blessed John Gummer, even before the local government elections were over.

Mr Major rose. 'Unlike you, I do not face senior members of my party emigrating to New Zealand!'

The Tories laughed and laughed at this reference to Bryan Gould, who is returning, not emigrating, to his native land.

As so often when watching sitcoms, one is most depressed by the energy and talent that went into producing such dross. Many highly paid people had sat in a room together, in Downing Street rather than Soho. After hours of thought and deliberation, that line was the best they could come up with.

Mr Smith said that public confidence in the government had broken down. Mr Major's script offered him no snappy comeback. Instead he listed the government's numerous achievements. A commercial break, I suppose.

Many of the funniest comedy shows work by exploiting the gap between human aspirations and life's tedious realities. Steptoe Jr, yearning for the cosmopolitan life, yet fated to be a rag and bone man all his days. Del Boy and Arthur Daley, always on the brink of the coup which will make them rich. Hyacinth Bucket (pronounced 'Bouquet') in *Keeping Up Appearances*, hungering for a social status which her situation will never quite permit.

The joke is that they never give up. We, the viewers, can see that they cannot win, but it wouldn't be funny if they realized it too. We laugh at them, but simultaneously we sympathize with their broken dreams.

If this government had a title, *Keeping Up Appearances* wouldn't be a bad one. (The brother-in-law with the pot belly and the string vest could be played by David Evans.) They long to be a real government and take real decisions. It's just us, sitting at home, whose strained hilarity reflects our knowledge that they will never quite make it.

4 May 1994

Innumerable readers (two) have written to complain about my slighting reference to Jeremy Irons. They say that he is a fine actor who uses understatement and nuance to convey more meaning than a blustering old ham like Donald Wolfit and that to compare him with David Evans MP is harsh and unfair.

Phooey. Did you see the film *Damage*? In the climactic scene, Mr Irons, playing an improbably taciturn government minister, is on the top floor of a big house, in bed – indeed in mid-bonk – with his own son's fiancée.

The son, whose suspicions have been alerted, comes upon them. Aghast, he staggers back and crashes over the balustrade on to the marble floor below. The naked Jeremy Irons hurtles down the stairs to cradle his dead son in his arms. In ten seconds his life and career have been destroyed for ever. The alert viewer can just detect him raising an eyebrow.

Understatement? I'd say that Jeremy Irons does for acting what rigor mortis does for ballet.

However, a colleague suggests that he might be useful to play Michael Portillo in a film about the fall of John Major. It's not a bad idea. Brian Glover could be Ken Clarke. For Heseltine, I would propose Wolfit himself, except that he is dead, so we may have to settle for the more obvious choice, Joanna Lumley.

One of the curiosities of the Commons is the way that, while great events are going on behind the scenes, nothing of them is visible on the floor of the House.

Douglas Hurd, who once even ran for the leadership *in public* was answering questions on foreign affairs. Few people talk about Mr Hurd as a future prime minister any more, possibly because he already has a starring role in *True Brits*, on the BBC.

This is called a documentary but is in fact a popular soap opera set in a seedy London street (Whitehall). It's filled with a variety of strong 'characters', and has already made a star of Tristan Garel-Jones, the louche, debonair, chain-smoking hunk who has been described as 'ten pounds of sex appeal in a five-pound bag'.

If the trend continues, we will have lurid tabloid articles about ministers' tangled love lives, their outrageous financial demands and their terror at being written out of the script. Actually, we already do, so nothing much will change.

Outside the Press Gallery I found a pile of copies of the speech to be delivered by the chancellor of the exchequer. It was headed: 'Clarke charts the changing world of work in the 1990s', so it was clearly a leadership bid. That's the most bewildering thing about these allegedly ferocious contests. MPs talk about turning the prime minister's back into a 'knife rack' (Tony Banks on Tuesday) but it isn't like that. There are no machine guns, no men in cloaks carrying bombs marked 'Bomb'. Instead ministers murmur about the future of a single European currency, or make speeches including lines such as 'I believe that a strong welfare state can complement, not hinder, more flexible markets ...'

That's about as ruthless as it gets. However, I did see one naked leadership bid in the Chamber, during the debate on the army. It was smooth, polished, articulate and carefully argued.

Nevertheless, as Menzies Campbell, the Liberal Democrat spokesman on defence has said several times, we don't need another Scottish advocate leading a political party. So Paddy Ashdown is safe for the time being.

(Soon after this column appeared, I received a card from someone who worked closely with Jeremy Irons on the film *Damage*. He said: 'If you think his performance was wooden in that, you should catch him in *The House of the Spirits*, with a Chilean accent which comes out as mid-Glamorgan.'

A month or so later I saw Irons appear as himself on the American chat show *Late Night with David Letterman*. To my surprise he was rather twitchy, wriggled in his seat, and created a wide range of exaggerated facial expressions. It struck me that his blank screen persona must be a greater indication of his acting talents than I had guessed.)

5 May 1994

It takes some guts to show your face in the House of Commons after the events at the end of last week. The horrible newspaper coverage, even fiercer in the Tory press than on the other side. The sheer scale of the humiliation. The knowledge that your colleagues are whispering behind your back, asking how long you can struggle on. The creeping fear that a once dazzling political career is about to reach its end.

So there was no sign of the prime minister. But Michael Brown did come into the Chamber, in spite of the weekend's tabloid allegations that he had had sex with an under-age youth. Mr Brown denies this and is taking legal action against the paper which printed it.

However, it is interesting to note that while not a single Tory MP has so far 'come out' as a homosexual (and only one Labour MP), these days there is no political price to pay for being friendly with someone alleged to be gay. So Mr Brown got a specially warm welcome. One would like to imagine this was because MPs were anxious to show sympathy for a member of a once-despised minority. In fact, it probably has more to do with solidarity against the press.

I can understand this. If we journalists were held to the same standards which we appear to insist upon for our elected representatives, there wouldn't be anyone left to write the newspapers. But fearful MPs know, as the Book of Numbers almost tells them, 'Be sure your *Sun* will find you out.'

Mr Brown arrived and chatted amiably with various of his colleagues, including Tristan Garel-Jones, Olga Maitland, Peter Bottomley, and more surprisingly, David Evans, the loud, right-wing Tory MP for Welwyn who is, by some freak of history, a member of the 1922 Committee Executive.

Mr Evans – or Husband of Janice, as he would no doubt like us to think of him – has a pretty consistent record of voting against gays at one time or another and would probably, if you asked him, also complain about the namby-pamby attitude of the Singapore authorities towards hooliganism.

All of which may give Mr Major some hope. In the old days, he might have expected round about now a deputation from the 1922 Executive, vast double-barrelled landowners swathed in worsted, gruff men who would regard sacking a prime minister as marginally less painful than dismissing their gamekeeper.

As it is, a large part of the '22 these days is comprised of essentially comic figures, such as Mr Evans, Rhodes Boyson, Marcus Fox and Jill Knight. A delegation from that lot would be no more terrifying than having the frighteners put on you by Arthur Daley.

But so many MPs seem to be ludicrous in one way or another. The likes of Geoffrey Dickens, Harry Greenway and Gyles Brandreth joined Lady Olga and Mr Evans in the Chamber. It seemed to be the Twilight of the *Garagistes*. David Davis, the young minister for the civil service, was answering questions. Senior figures in the party – if there can be said to be such people – are already tipping him as the Next-Tory-Leader-But-Two. Poor sod.

10 May 1994

In mid-May the Disabled Persons (Civil Rights) Bill
came to the floor of the House, where its progress was
slowed to a crawl by a large number of amendments,
mostly tabled by Lady Olga Maitland. Supporters of the
bill, on both sides of the House, suspected that Lady
Olga had been put up to this by the government, which
believed that the bill would be far too costly for industry,
though the figures were widely disputed. The suspicion
was that ministers wished to wreck the bill's prospects
but did not want the opprobrium of appearing to vote
against handicapped people. However, Nicholas Scott,
the minister concerned, denied that his department had
drafted the amendments. It turned out that this was not
true.

You may have seen the painting of John Major unveiled
by his wife, Norma, at the National Portrait Gallery this
week. It shows him leaning on a library cabinet, glancing
up from a book with a light perhaps sardonic smile
playing about his lips.

The artist, Peter Deighan, has cunningly composed the
portrait so that the viewer's eye is drawn inexorably to the
prime minister's trousers. (You can tell it's great art when
the pants follow you round the room.) In Mr Major's case
these are dramatically creased around the upper leg.

Rumpled Crotch Syndrome (RCS) is something most
men suffer from, though rarely to quite this extent. Fans
of Steve Bell's cartoon strip in the *Guardian* will guess the
reason why, though the famous Y-fronts would have to be
made of hot corrugated iron to have this effect. Or he
might have been playing pocket billiards with a real cue.

Naturally I had a good look at the premier's zippered
regions yesterday afternoon, and it seemed to me that his
trousers were pretty well pressed – on the Michael Foot
scale of RCS, they would rate no worse than a 3. He also
seemed fairly relaxed and confident, even acknowledging
Labour's deafening and sarcastic cheers with a smile.

Perhaps Mr Deighan has, with an artist's insight, used

the trousers to suggest Mr Major's inner turmoil, a contrast to the smooth, calm face he presents to the public – the Daks of Dorian Grey, perhaps.

The whips had done their work, and the day's first question was a lickspittle query about Britain's industrial growth. The prime minister's trousers hung sharp and crisp.

Then Mr Smith asked him about a referendum on Europe: was he proposing to hold one? Mr Major was purposefully vague. He was 'sceptical'. The question 'does not arise', and if it ever did, 'it doesn't need to be decided now'. What was more, he would never present an 'unacceptable package' to the House. William Empson's famous work of literary criticism is called *Seven Types of Ambiguity*. If he'd studied John Major, he'd have had to make it 57 varieties at least.

As always, when Mr Major evades a question, he goes on to imply that he has actually answered it with uncompromising directness. Mr Smith got no further, and the prime minister sat down with his trousers as neatly ironed as if they had just popped out of one of those presses they leave you in hotel rooms, which put in a crease almost exactly parallel to the one already there.

Then Nicholas Scott rose to make a personal statement. He admitted that he had 'misled' the House over the government's killing of the disabled rights bill. Oddly enough, while accusing an MP of lying is not permitted in the House, lying itself seems to be all right provided you call it 'misleading'.

My hope was that Mr Scott, who is a popular man, would follow the advice of his daughter Victoria, a lobbyist for disabled people, and resign in protest against himself. He could then run against Mr Major in the autumn. He might even win. But he had certainly been telling porkies last Friday – not run-of-the-mill mini-porkettes, but cartwheel-sized Melton Mowbray pies with extra jelly.

There must be a picture of him somewhere in very baggy trousers.

(Steve Bell, the *Guardian*'s popular political cartoonist, began drawing Major with his underpants over his trousers in late 1990, shortly after he had become prime minister. The idea was to remind readers of Superman's smart blue briefs, though, Bell thought, Major would wear Marks and Spencer aertex Y-fronts instead. By a coincidence items began to appear in the political gossip columns about what appeared to be a curious sartorial habit of the prime minister's. Flying abroad on one occasion, he went to the back of the plane to chat to the press. As he bent down, someone noticed through the gap opened at the back of his trousers that he appeared to have tucked his shirt tails into his underpants. Whether he actually does this as a matter of morning routine, we don't know; some theories hold that he wears those beltless trousers which have elastic inside the waist band, and that has created the confusion. In any event, Bell's image, for many people, *is* John Major.

The day described above was John Smith's last appearance at Prime Minister's Question Time.)

11 May 1994

I have changed my mind and decided that it would have been outrageous for Nicholas Scott to have been forced to resign his office for lying to the House of Commons. All ministers lie to the House of Commons. Why should he be singled out?

Some of their lies are not particularly serious, the equivalent of murmuring 'delicious' to your hostess at the end of an inedible meal. But there does seem to me a culture of easy mendacity in this government, a spivvish sense that it doesn't much matter what you say provided you can get away with it. Ministers resemble those chaps who sell £20 Rolexes in Oxford Street, who probably also spend little time pondering the morality of what they do. In a way, one has the greater contempt for the people who are naïve or greedy enough to believe what they claim.

That said, Mr Scott can count himself lucky that he is still in paid employment. Here a little Leavisite textual analysis is necessary.

On Friday, the minister denied that the 80 amendments which blocked the private member's Disabled Persons (Civil Rights) Bill were the work of his officials: 'No part whatever has been taken in the drafting of any amendments, and to the best of my knowledge, nobody in my department has been involved in the drafting of any amendments in this area.'

On Tuesday, having been caught bang to rights, he apologized: 'My statement on Friday that my department had not drafted any amendments was true, but, as I explained in a letter ... the department, with my authority, had been involved in their preparation.

'I therefore felt that I should offer this clarification of my remarks ...'

Hmmm. I can see that word 'clarification' becoming quite a popular euphemism. What Mr Scott has done is assert that he was accurate on a single narrow point – his claim that officials had not actually *drafted* the amendments. This ringing declaration of his own honesty then allows him to slide around the whopper ('nobody in my department has been involved ...') with the weasel word 'clarification'.

Wife: You told me you were working late, but you've

got lipstick all over your shirt. You were with that little trollop, weren't you? Don't lie to me.

Husband: When I said that I was working late, that was perfectly true. In that subsequently I did take my secretary out to dinner and then on to a cheap hotel room, my remarks may have been inadvertently misleading, and I am happy to offer you this clarification.

Yesterday Betty Boothroyd infuriated Labour MPs by saying that she would not take the matter any further, since the House was 'now in full possession of the facts, and has received an apology'.

Members rose to point out that anyone could now fib their heads off if they were merely prepared to say 'sorry' when they were caught – if they were caught. But in my view it would be best for Mr Scott to stay in office. He is a competent and well-liked minister and, no doubt whatever legislation the government does serve up to cover its own blushes will, no doubt, be better for being worked upon by Mr Scott.

At the same time, paradoxically, his continued presence in the government is a useful symbol of its dishonesty and arrogance, a permanent reminder of ministers' contempt for both the public and the House of Commons.

12 May 1994

As it happens, Mr Scott was fired in the July government reshuffle. It seemed a good example of everyone getting the worst of all worlds. Mr Scott was a capable fellow, so his dismissal must have been the result of his misleading the House. But didn't his secretary of state, Peter Lilley, know and agree with the strategy? What about the Leader of the House? And if what Mr Scott did was so wicked that it merited sacking, why was he not fired at the time, instead of two months later? If Mr Scott had followed my initial advice at the time and resigned, he would have been in just the same position he found himself unwillingly in July, but would appear as one of the few honourable men left in British politics.

It must have been especially bitter for him to be replaced as minister of state in the Department of Social Security by Mr William Hague, a young shaver of 33, who is rising towards the top with astonishing speed and is clearly set to be the country's youngest cabinet minister, assuming the Tory government lasts that long.

The notion of Mr Hague having a direct influence on my life is rather frightening, since I have never been able to take him seriously. In 1977, while still a teenager, he spoke to the Conservative Party conference, appearing at the rostrum soon after the representatives had watched, fascinated, as the mighty structure of Michael Heseltine's hair collapsed. I dug round in the archives to find what I'd written about this whippersnapper at the time. It was rather like the process of finding the new Dalai Lama: one felt that the Thatcher strawberry mark had been discovered on his bottom at a very early age:

> One young man who had obviously had his hair heseltined for the day was a 16-year-old from the Rother Valley called William Hague. One hesitates to say too much about the young men at this Tory conference, except that there are an awful lot of them and they are terrifyingly confident. Young William had a surprisingly elderly-sounding Yorkshire accent, which made his voice sound almost exactly like Harold Wilson's, to the obvious confusion of delegates who had their backs turned.
>
> He had, however, a far greater command of cliché than the former prime minister, and he marked the

economic debate with phrases such as 'rolling back the frontiers of the state', 'home-owning democracy', 'large and progressive cuts in public spending', and 'a society where effort and initiative are rewarded'. The sight of these aged saws coming from so young a head had the entire conference on its feet.

The most disconcerting thing of all was that William did not even look surprised as Mrs Thatcher herself leaned over from the platform to applaud him. He merely seemed faintly pleased, as if he had won the hundred-yard dash, or the school prize for diligence.

13 October 1977

John Smith died on the morning of the 12 May. He had attended a gala fund-raising dinner the previous evening, another Luvvies for Labour function at which people had paid huge sums for the privilege of sitting near shadow cabinet ministers and various show-business people.

Perhaps the formal announcement was most affecting. At exactly 2.33 the House was jammed, not with its usual ragged sprawl, but as if MPs were already at the funeral, sitting stiffly upright, the rowdy benches turned briefly into pews.

Betty Boothroyd said very simply: 'I regret to have to report to the House the death of the Right Honourable John Smith, QC, member for Monklands East.' It seemed touch and go whether she would reach the end without breaking down.

On the Labour benches several people were crying, and some of those were men. Others had that blank stare we associate with war hospitals. Neil Kinnock and John

Prescott gazed straight ahead but they were clearly not seeing anything.

Outside the Chamber male Labour MPs hugged each other. Others were blotchy and red-eyed, clutching handkerchiefs. Sometimes they scurried along with their heads down, avoiding eye contact with anyone else.

I don't recall seeing the whole House of Commons grieve before. Some deaths are profoundly shocking, like Airey Neave's murder, but this time the mood was sober and raw, a dead weight of unhappiness. I was reminded of the hours after the Brighton bomb.

A Tory rushed by me, a florid right-winger famous for his attacks on Smith. 'This has knocked the guts out of this place,' he said. But MPs never quite stop plotting. This is not hypocrisy; it's in their nature. 'It's certainly bought time for John Major,' another Tory right-winger said sarcastically, 'perhaps as much as a week.'

At 3.30 they came back for the tributes. Christian funeral observances move from the pain of the burial, on to the lighter mood of the wake, which becomes a celebration of the life that is gone. Somehow the Commons managed to reflect the same progress, as the sense of loss mingled with an outpouring of affection.

The prime minister was open, generous, even humorous. If Mr Major managed anything else with so sure a touch, he'd be unchallenged. He called Smith one of the outstanding modern parliamentarians, fair minded, 'and a tough fighter for what he believed in ... on good days – for him there were many good days – his speeches could shape and move the will of the House.'

He seemed genuinely affected. John Smith was, he said, a man without malice. After a dispute, there were 'no bruises'. And it was hard to bear knowing that we would never see his debating skills again. They had often clashed in the House but met in private later. 'Again, no bruises.'

'We would share a drink, sometimes tea – and sometimes not tea,' and often the discussions had strayed from the subject and over the scheduled time. 'When I think of John Smith, I think of an opponent, not an enemy.' He spoke about a waste, of political talent, of a high and honourable ambition to lead the country, of the happiness he would have deserved in retirement.

Normally when the House of Commons is said to be at its best, it is actually at its worst. For once they got it right.

The leader of the Labour Party rose. The move from misery to commemoration was underway. Smith had been 'no sobersides. He had a wicked sense of humour'. She had seen a childhood photo of him in a Just William pose, shirt tails out, and tie up around his ear. 'Those who saw him every day had no difficulty in detecting that boy in the statesman and leader.' Yet he had a natural strength: 'I have never known a man so at ease with himself.' His last words in public had been impromptu, at Wednesday's gala dinner. 'The opportunity to serve our country – that is all we ask.' Let it, she said, stand as his epitaph.

Neil Kinnock, whose reputation has soared since Tories always like a socialist who no longer threatens them, quoted Shelley: 'He burst the icy chains of custom, and shone, a day star of his age.' At the end the Speaker called Dennis Skinner, who is almost a part of our constitution by now. He wanted the House to pass the disabled rights bill unanimously, as a tribute.

Labour MPs let their tension out in laughter. At first I thought Skinner's remarks tasteless, personal grandstanding. But then I thought not. John Smith knew you had to be partisan to achieve anything. So a mini-rant from Skinner made a good tribute too.

13 May 1994

A tribute to Smith also appeared the day after his death.

The image of a dour Presbyterian lawyer could hardly have been more wrong. What John Smith liked was what the Irish call the 'crack', that blend of companionship, booze, atmosphere and wit which can lift a conversation into an evanescent work of art.

He was one of the sharpest and funniest men I've met. You'd be having an ordinary political chat, and suddenly the zinger would come out of the sun. 'Margaret Beckett? Proof that the Rehabilitation of Offenders Act does work …' The tributes said that he was without malice. That's not true; every successful politician is malicious, but in his case it was genial and amiable, a constructive malice.

In 1982 I caught a sleeper from Glasgow and saw his name on the manifest. He appeared at the cabin door clanking with miniatures acquired from a friendly steward. Two minutes later there was another knock, and a Scottish Nationalist MP appeared, pulling from what was clearly a remarkable back trouser pocket an entire bottle of whisky.

The conversation was gossipy, funny and exceedingly malicious, the more so because Scottish politics makes a snake pit look like – yes – a vicarage tea party. I got rid of them at Rugby, an hour north of London. Of course as I tottered out on to the platform at Euston I could not, through the hangover, remember a word of what had been said.

After his 1988 heart attack he did cut down considerably on both food and drink. Articles appeared describing an intake which included lashings of bran cereal and skimmed milk. But it was, frankly, rare to see Smith at a party with a glass of skimmed milk in his hand. I suspect he shared the delusion that dry white wine is a non-alcoholic drink.

Like all lawyers, he had a store of good legal anecdotes. One of his favourites was about his early days at the Bar when he had to defend a particularly unpleasant 15-year-old hooligan. The solicitor, a large man who had fought in the Spanish Civil War – for Franco – addressed the youth: 'I have managed to obtain, at considerable expense, the services of one of the most eminent advocates at the Scottish Bar, a junior who is undoubtedly destined for high office. So sit in the corner, you wee cunt, and listen to what he says.'

The pose as a boring bank manager was deliberate. Partly it was his background: that was how people in authority were supposed to behave. Partly it was because, just as John Major had won an election by being the un-Thatcher, he wanted to be the un-Kinnock. But he was also comfy with the style. His political heroes, he said, were Attlee and Truman, both unshowy men who preferred getting the work done.

In the sonorous cliché which everyone used yesterday, he was a great House of Commons man. Just as Willie Sutton robbed banks 'because that's where the money is', Smith worked in Parliament because that's where the power is.

Innumerable times you'd see him bustling around, 'steaming down the Committee Corridor like a small rhinoceros', as one of his colleagues said.

But there was also rage inside there. Beneath the studious and owlish blink of his public appearances, there was a real hatred of this government. The constant criticism of him by Labour activists, that he had no fire in his belly, was mistaken. He believed it was absolutely essential to get the present lot out, and that everything, including his own natural inclinations, had to be subordinate to that great cause.

For example, I and other journalists wrote that he should have used his wit more against John Major. I felt that the leader of the Opposition didn't have to be an imitation prime minister; it was his job to lampoon the sitting incumbent, for his wit to crystallize the country's sense of anger and betrayal. But he said privately that it was essential that he behaved with stern gravitas. 'I must always appear statesmanlike,' he said insistently.

I am sure that is why he often seemed stilted and slow-footed at Question Time; he was often holding back the bubble of high spirits. When he could relax and expand, he was a superb parliamentary performer, one of the few left in the House. In the meantime, he seemed to want to out-grey Major. As a Tory minister said recently, 'If John Smith were to replace John Major, do you think the financial markets would even notice?'

Yesterday the prime minister painted a picture of the two men, convivial and at ease over a behind-the-scenes drink, as their private offices anxiously wondered why the meeting was lasting so long. Smith himself felt differently; he didn't especially dislike Major; but had little time or affection for him. 'There's nothing to like or dislike there,' he once said. But he hated the sleaze and corruption which has clung to this government, if not personally to its leader. He detested the crookery, the lies, the petty evasions and the featherbedding of rich friends and Tory contributors. He was infuriated by the Nicholas Scott affair, an act of deceit which went against everything he felt about the duties imposed by public life. As his friend Menzies Campbell said yesterday, 'He had all the virtues of a Scottish Presbyterian, but none of the vices.'

Well, precious few. I have never known the Commons have the genuine sense of grief we saw yesterday.

13 May 1994

Mr Smith's death began a strangely quiet period, in which the normal hostilities were suspended until after his funeral.

My favourite Questions session, to the Parliamentary Spokesman for the Church Commissioners, came round again. Simon Hughes asked about asset management of the Church Commissioners' land. Apparently the commissioners, who have lost hundreds of millions of pounds in ill-advised speculation, keep erecting luxury houses on their land in the hopes of recovering the money.

Mr Hughes felt they should build less expensive dwellings for ordinary people, since Jesus never said: 'Upon this rock I shall build executive maisonettes.'

The next question had been tabled by Mr Tony Banks, who wriggled with pleasure as his moment approached. But the Second Church Estates Commissioner, Mr Michael Alison of Selby, gets only five minutes of glory a month, so undercutting even Andy Warhol. The time was up; Mr Banks looked cross, and we moved on to questions from the parliamentary secretary to the Lord Chancellor, John Taylor. Mr Taylor looks like a plump little Birmingham solicitor, which is what he is.

However, his skills were hardly required, since only two of the seven MPs who had tabled questions bothered to show up (increasingly Mondays are becoming another day off for MPs, giving them a four-day weekend).

As he reached the last question with ten minutes still to go, Mr Taylor said: 'I had better read this fairly slowly.'

Mr Banks perked up. 'You're not being paid by the word now!' he shouted.

Mr Taylor replied, somewhat gloomily, 'I am actually speaking without a fee for the first time in my life.'

Even a lawyer billing by the hour could not stretch out a single answer for ten minutes, so by the rules of order we went back to the Church Commissioners and Mr Banks.

'There is a God!' he yelled in glee.

This is a question which has vexed scholars, philosophers and theologians since the Dawn of Man. But no one has yet suggested that His existence can be determined by the number of times Mr Banks gets to ask a parliamentary question.

It was about church security. Mr Banks started quite normally. Though he was not himself religious, he said, he felt that robbing churches was distasteful and a breach of trust. Then he went loopy. There ought to be a specialized group within the police which concentrated entirely on this type of crime: 'a police version of the Spanish Inquisition'.

The implication that the police should use red hot pokers and the rack to extract confessions from people who steal lead would obviously please many Tory MPs, especially Mr Terry Dicks, who told the authorities in Qatar to go ahead with the flogging of a young British man whom they accused of trafficking in alcohol. But then in Mr Dicks's ideal world, no doubt crime and punishment would be privatized and sold off to the government of Qatar, who would soon put a dent in football hooliganism, and indeed in football hooligans.

Mr Alison replied: 'The founder of the Christian religion did warn us not to lay up our treasures upon earth, where moth and rust doth corrupt, and where thieves break through and steal ... lay up yourself treasure in Heaven (Matthew vi.19).'

As a crime policy, this has more promise than some of Mr Howard's recent ideas. 'Not a lot we can do, sir. I suggest you keep your jewellery and credit cards in Heaven where these young lads can't get at 'em.'

17 May 1994

English slang is remarkably speedy. Tony Blair is not yet leader of the Labour Party – he isn't even a candidate so far – but already he has a shiny new nickname, 'Bambi'. I suppose this refers to his big, trusting eyes, and is meant to be pejorative.

But Bambi, far from being a cervine wimp who spent his time talking to flowers and bunny rabbits, went on to become Prince of the Forest, thanks in part to his great slogan: 'Tough on hunting, tough on the causes of hunting.'

Either way, Mr Blair was not around for Prime Minister's Questions yesterday. Nor was Gordon Brown. Margaret Beckett, now leader of the Labour Party, was obliged to be there, and John Prescott had been around for Employment Questions, but none of the other candidates could be seen. They were hiding. Even sitting silently on a bench before John Smith's funeral could have cost vital votes.

In the meantime, the weird truce between the parties continued. Both sides were courteous, reasonable and constructive. It was a horrible vision of how the public imagines it wants its politicians to behave.

For one thing, they aren't any good at being reasonable and constructive – they employ people to be those for them. Saying they should be courteous is like saying the Queen ought to do a bit more housework; it's not what she's there for.

When the prime minister walked in, there wasn't even a sarcastic cheer from the Labour benches. Mrs Beckett inquired about a report on seat belts in buses. When would it be published? Mr Major said soon. Mrs Beckett hoped it would be very soon. Mr Major said it would come any day now. Mrs Beckett said there should be a bill about it.

Max Madden asked about someone who is being held without trial in a Pakistani prison. Mr Major said that he would have a word with the government of Pakistan. Mr Madden thanked him warmly for his help.

Bruce Grocott raised the situation in Rwanda. MPs agreed that it was terrible. 'Unforgivable,' Mr Major added.

We got on to war widows. MPs felt they had made 'remarkable sacrifices'. The campaign against breast cancer? 'Important'.

Peter Luff tried to win a Greasy Spoon for asking about the prospects for the soaraway British economy but Mr Major wasn't falling for that. He grinned broadly as he said: 'The prospects for the economy are extremely good.'

He was about to read out one of his Lists of Heartening Statistics but he couldn't even bring himself to do that. 'I will spare you all the rest of what it says here,' he ended.

'That were boring,' said Mr Skinner. To be fair, he had tried to end the truce single-handedly by denouncing an employment minister's answer as 'a pack of lies'.

Madam Speaker: 'Did I hear you correctly? It was "a pack of lies"?'

Mr Skinner: 'I was using the collective noun.'

Which, if you think about it, was a meaningless answer. But the grisly mood of bi-partisanship extended even to the relationship between Skinner and the Speaker, who decided to let him off.

This has been awful. Hostilities should resume within five days at the very latest.

18 May 1994

This mood did not, thankfully, last very long. Expecting MPs to be courteous to each other is as pointless as telling Dennis the Menace to sit quietly and be a good boy.

After the shock of last week, the House of Commons is showing some signs of recovery. The patient is sitting up in bed and has managed a little warm milk. Children are still being asked not to play near the bedroom, the curtains remain drawn, but the House has watched a little daytime TV (*Good Morning with Anne and Nick* to be specific, which is always a mistake. Anne Diamond's response to the events of last week was to say that 'John Smith was a man with a great heart.')

I see the House as a not very lovable curmudgeon, whose recovery will be signalled when he resumes abusing the staff. I was reminded of a friend of mine who had a difficult relationship with his mother. He found himself in hospital with a life-threatening illness. Once his mother visited him at the same time as a group of his friends. He rose stiffly from his pillow and let out a stream of abuse at the old lady.

Her eyes brimmed with tears. The friends gathered round to comfort her. 'No, no, you don't understand,' she said, 'these are tears of joy. He must be getting better!'

In the same way, some of us in the Press Gallery had to dab a thoughtful eye when Tony Baldry, the environment minister, accused Gordon Prentice of talking 'absolute twaddle'. Not a clever remark, hardly likely to win the *Observer* Mace, but a warming sign of life.

Then there was a truly greasy question to John Gummer, the environment secretary, who is someone I like personally in spite of his resemblance in public to a margarine sandwich, being bland, oily and unpalatable. (By the way, did you see that the makers of Flora margarine are to change their recipe, having accepted, according to *The Times*, 'growing scientific evidence that the trans-fatty acids in their product could be as dangerous as the saturated fats in butter'.

Flora! The gruesome stuff which we have been urged to eat for years instead of the honest products of nature's bounty! The lesson is that we should not believe any scientific scare story for at least 25 years and should never accept their crackpot solutions, whether it's for the ozone layer, or the 'eggs, milk and butter will kill you' scam.)

Sorry. Just wanted to get that off my chest. The greasy question to Gummer came from Rod Richards and it concerned investment by the new water companies. Apparently this has trebled.

This glad news (if it's true, why does our tap water still taste like a Haitian swimming pool?) was not enough for Mr Richards. He asked, 'Is the minister aware that recently I opened a new sewage treatment plant in my constituency and will my honourable friends come to sunny Rhyl so they can swim in the beautiful clean sea with their families?'

It was all too much for one Labour MP. Forgetting the truce, forgetting that his own leader would not be in the ground for another 48 hours, he let out a heartfelt: 'What a load of crap!' It was grand to see the House on the mend.

19 May 1994

The reason why otherwise sane persons like Mr Richards are prepared to grovel publicly in this odious fashion is that it does work. Just two months after he asked his question in praise of the new water companies (and in the midst of public disquiet about both the size of their bills and the emoluments paid to their chief executives) Mr Richards was made a minister at the Welsh Office, displacing Sir Wyn Roberts, who had been in government since 1979.

The next day, as reported below, another young crawler called Simon Burns asked a similarly oleaginous question. He too was promoted to ministerial office as an assistant whip.

Two minutes before he was due to begin, the prime minister tried to make his way to the Despatch Box. Unfortunately his path was blocked by the colossal figure of Nicholas Soames, the food minister. Mr Soames did not see his boss and assumed that the loud cheers were for him.

He beamed and bowed satirically. MPs on both sides roared. The prime minister's route was still impeded. In desperation he placed a hand on Mr Soames's bottom. It was a friendly, collegiate hand, no more, but its arrival caused the most terrible embarrassment.

I was sitting immediately above Mr Soames, and was able to study his bald head as it coped with the enormity of his mistake. First his scalp turned pink, then scarlet, vermilion, magenta, and finally the deepest, the richest, the most purple hue I have ever seen upon a human being. It was a wondrous colour, as dark as a ripe merlot grape, as lustrous as a coronation gown.

Given the astonishing set of arteries, veins, capillaries and sheer *plumbing* that created this effect – within perhaps no more than five seconds – it must truly be counted one of Nature's miracles. It had vanished within a minute, but like the aurora borealis, or Halley's comet, it was an unforgettable phenomenon which I shall one day describe to my grandchildren.

The week's Greasy Spoon award went to Simon Burns of Chelmsford, who prefaced a lickspittle question about the 'steady and sustainable recovery' with the phrase: 'If my right honourable friend will forgive me for changing the subject ...' These creepy little curlicues score heavily with the judges, Mr Burns – keep it up.

Mr Heseltine made his statement on the privatization of the Post Office. It has become a rather whiskery joke that sooner or later the government would privatize the monarchy, and we would have the Everest Double Glazing Royal Family or Her Majesty the Cornhill Assurance Queen Mother. What we didn't realize was that something along those lines is now likely to happen.

Mr Heseltine explained that the new, private post office would continue to be called the Royal Mail, I suppose in the same sense that there is a Royal Tandoori in Notting Hill. The stamps will also keep the Queen's head as a logo, like the brewery ads on cricketers' pullovers.

As Patrick Cormack put it, the whole idea was as acceptable as the Guards being replaced at Buckingham Palace by Group 4.

20 May 1994

After terrible defeats in the local elections, the Conservatives tried as hard as they could to avert a similar disaster in June's elections for the European Parliament. These days, however, what counts in elections is not how well you do, but how well you do compared to what the press and the polls have predicted. So, although the Tories took only 18 seats – a catastrophically poor performance – this was better than the single figures which had been predicted in some quarters. The Conservatives claimed a mighty victory and the received wisdom changed its mind about John Major's survival.

The prime minister slipped into Bristol unannounced yesterday to give the first big speech of the Tories' election campaign. Holders of the precious tickets (it is easier for a camel to enter Centre Court at Wimbledon than for a voter to get into a modern political meeting) had not even known until the weekend that Mr Major was to come amongst them.

Even the passes only promised a '1994 European Election Event', a billing which would put off all but the most diehard fans.

These were the solid Tory bedrock. There is something impressively enduring about them. If you compared them to the same gathering 30 years ago, I doubt if, apart from a single turbaned Sikh, you would have noticed much difference at all – the men with toothbrush moustaches and loud, check tweeds, the floral dresses and hats, the youths who wear suits even when they're not at work, all with that determined gleam in the eye. These people are tough. They are used to getting their own way. They will never desert the Tories. We may laugh at them but we should never underestimate them.

Sir Norman Fowler arrived on stage to a sprinkling of applause. The Conservatives' strategy was immediately clear – once again they are running against their traditional enemy, Lady Thatcher.

'Since John Major became prime minister, inflation has fallen from 11 per cent to 2.6 per cent. We have moved out of recession to a growth rate of 2 per cent a year, the fastest in Yurp [sic] ... if we had said that those things would be achieved when John Major became prime minister, no one would have believed us.'

Eleven years of Tory misrule would make a good slogan for the Labour Party; it's a bold move for the Conservatives to use it as well.

Mr Major finally arrived. For a man said to be facing a last, terrible election campaign, he looked remarkably relaxed. He was, if not at the end of his tether, perhaps half way down his tether, whatever that means. There were no personal attacks. The man he called 'Monsieur Oui, the poodle of Brussels' is now dead, and even if he himself is running as Herr Nein, the Dobermann of Huntingdon, he is loath to attack anyone else.

I was reminded of the American joke about the shipwreck victims who are all eaten by sharks, except for the lawyers. When asked why, they said: 'professional courtesy'.

Whenever politicians go on tour, the most entertaining part of their speeches is usually not for the national TV cameras but for local consumption. It is designed to make each town or region feel its qualities are uniquely important to the nation. You can gauge how sincere these tributes are by asking how it would sound if they were to imply the opposite elsewhere.

For example, Mr Major said: 'People in the West Country are individualists. Independent minded. Tough, proud people who know what they want, and are not afraid to say so.

'For generation after generation they have worked and fought, and sometimes died to make this nation what it is.'

Now, do you think that if Mr Major goes to, say, Norwich later in the campaign, he will say: 'People in East Anglia are conformists, followers of the herd. Weak, feeble-minded folk who have little idea of what they want and would be too timid to ask for it if they did.

'For generations they have skulked, hiding from their country's call'? Of course not.

24 May 1994

Yesterday was the turn of Robin Cook's leadership bid, and it could not have been more effective. He trashed Michael Heseltine. Admittedly this was made fairly easy by an extraordinary fact: Mr Heseltine made a boring speech. Or rather, he read out a boring statement. It was about a new White Paper on competitiveness and it was stupendously, thunderously boring. It was so boring that it was, in its way, quite fascinating.

(My colleagues and I used to have a running debate about the most boring man in Britain who, we naturally assumed, must be an MP. We switched our search to the second most boring man in Britain, since the most boring man would, in a perverse way, be quite an interesting figure. He has since lost his seat.)

On and on Mr Heseltine droned. Wide-ranging reviews followed focal points. Initiatives were extended and partnerships enhanced. One mind-numbing abstraction was plonked on top of another and mortared into place. It all induced a faintly claustrophobic panic, as if we were about to be walled up with words.

Labour MPs began to enjoy the surprising spectacle and shouted out: 'Author! Author!' Betty Boothroyd said she would be obliged if the House would settle down. In the brief pause which followed, Mr Heseltine resumed: 'Madam Speaker, local sources of innovation support ...' Labour MPs couldn't help themselves and erupted all over again.

After a while they began to notice that the statement promised an awful lot of consultation and very little action. So when Mr Heseltine declared: 'We shall publish a White Paper on ...' they cheered uproariously. He said it again: 'We shall publish a White Paper!' They cheered louder.

'Order!' shouted the Speaker. 'It *is* a bit comical,' said one Labour hooligan in a high-pitched northern accent, reminiscent of the late Sandy Powell. 'We shall publish a White Paper!' said Hezza. When, finally, he uttered the word 'finally', the hilarity took minutes to subside.

You had to feel a little sorry for the president. After all, he didn't write the statement and he had no choice but to read it. It was as if Demosthenes were obliged to plough through the Macedonian phone book. As he sat down, Labour bayed out their final frantic cheers. Behind him his loyal PPS, Richard Ottaway, flapped a loyal but lonely order paper.

Mr Cook could hardly fail, and he didn't. He ran through the alternative statistics on the government's record (trade surplus now a huge deficit, investment halved, and so on) then into a well judged passage about the expense of the 'glitzy' White Paper itself, all accompanied by much document-play – disdainfully flipping through the thing, then letting it fall on the table like a discarded toy.

Then on to the peroration: 'A bankrupt government on the verge of liquidation ...' The Tories sat gloomily silent, the hurtling speed of Mr Cook's reply preventing them from inserting their own mockery which, like the Mexican wave at sports grounds, needs to gain momentum if it is to establish itself.

Unleashed from the civil service prose, Mr Heseltine's reply to the reply was magnificently, majestically over the top. The man who can always find the clitoris of the Tory Party was now shaking the windpipe of the Labour Party. As the rant gained in volume, Dennis Skinner and Terry Lewis sat tastefully patting their hearts.

25 May 1994

I decided to go channel-surfing, as the Americans say, around the Euro-election campaigns. At the Conservatives, the foreign secretary produced a surprise supporter, a well known Liberal who, it turned out, was adamantly opposed to the Social Chapter of the Maastricht Treaty.

His name was Bill. 'What on earth would Gladstone have made of the Social Chapter?' mused Mr Hurd. 'He would have recoiled in horror.'

This was a reference to William Ewart Gladstone (Lib Newark, Oxford, Lancashire South, Greenwich, and Midlothian – he changed constituencies as often as his party now changes its name). It's generally a sign that things are going badly when one party evokes in aid the dead leader of another party. You may recall the *Sun*'s scoop during the 1992 general election: 'Stalin backs Labour', based on the findings of a spiritualist who discovered that Mussolini too was supporting Neil Kinnock.

Over at the Liberals, Alex Carlile disagreed about Gladstone's views on the issue of the day. 'The Social Chapter is very Gladstonian,' he said. The LibDems' campaign leader Charles Kennedy looked mildly distressed. 'This is becoming the War of Gladstone's Tomb,' he said glumly.

Mr Carlile then changed the subject by producing a new word, a wonderfully resonant, Liberal kind of new word: 'potentiating'. Someone who didn't mind admitting their own ignorance asked what it meant. Mr Carlile explained: 'It means the giving of potential.'

Mr Kennedy looked more pained than ever. 'Potentiators for Gladstone – a new fringe group,' he groaned – and he was right to be upset. I see them now in their wispy beards and dirty trainers, pushing leaflets into delegates' hands. 'We in the PFG demand that the leadership potentiate us immediately ...'

I turned to Mr Gladstone's *oeuvre* to find out his true views on Europe. In 1888, speaking in Caernarvon, he declared: 'We are part of the community of Europe and must do our duty as such.' In the code of today that amounts to Euro-fanaticism on a scale which currently exists only in Ted Heath and Hugh Dykes. It was a snub for Mr Hurd and a victory for the potentiators.

Back at the Commons I asked a Labour MP about the national executive meeting which had just laid down the arrangements for the leadership election. 'It was wonderful to see the NEC so united about one individual,' they said. 'We all expressed our approval of a job well done, and gave him a pat on the back.'

This had to be a first for the most poisonous committee in British politics. However, the praise turned out to be for Offa, David Blunkett's seeing eye dog, who is now retiring. Everyone else got rubbished, as usual.

Unlike Lady Olga Maitland, who has been fibbing to the Commons about the disabled bill and her role in helping the government to block it. The Speaker said yesterday that she had 'fallen below the standards which the House is entitled to expect ... I strongly rebuke her.'

This is as strict as Betty gets, the parliamentary equivalent of having your sword broken over an officer's knee. But Lady Olga gets to keep her seat anyway. As I have said before, the crime in Parliament is not to lie, but to accuse someone else of lying, even when they are. Especially when they are.

Lady Olga replied: 'In the light of your statement, may I give an unreserved apology to you and this House?' (I liked her phrase: 'in the light of your statement', with its cunning suggestion that the offence would not have mattered if it had not been discovered.)

26 May 1994

The European elections were very bad indeed for the Conservatives, but slightly better than expected, so they were greeted as a tremendous triumph. Sir Norman Fowler, still chairman of the party, declared that the corner had been turned and the worst was over. Mr Major, perhaps imitating Bill Clinton's practice of holding al fresco press conferences, held a briefing in the garden of Number Ten. Among other plans, he promised a reshuffle of ministers, and suggested that Prime Minister's Question Time was in need of reform.

Prime Minister's Question Time does need reform. It needs reform like the Black Hole of Calcutta needed flying ducks on the wall – desirable in its way, but hardly meeting the situation.

Ideally, Prime Minister's Question Time would be abolished altogether and replaced by something more useful – short topical debates, perhaps, or the Chippendales. I doubt whether anything much will change. The twice-weekly session is as ghastly as it is because it suits too many people for it to stay that way.

Yesterday's exchanges were preceded by some mild black comedy as David Blunkett's new dog, a curly-coated retriever named Lucy, led him to the Despatch Box on the government side of the House. It was the MP himself who had to steer Lucy round in the right direction, the first instance of a dog being guided by a seeing eye Blunkett.

Then Mr Major arrived to massive cheers from the Tory benches, led by the minister who had been answering questions for the previous 45 minutes, John Patten. It is widely believed that Mr Patten is about to be ceremonially slaughtered on an Aztec altar to propitiate the gods of public opinion. So he felt it was not enough merely to cheer; he accompanied his huzzahs with an up-and-down chopping motion of his right hand, perhaps an old-fashioned way of encouraging the Light Blues along the towpath, but looking unnervingly like the familiar gesture very rude motorists make to slow drivers.

But the cheers were the loudest Mr Major has received recently. It takes a remarkable amount of chutzpah to turn the worst result ever suffered by the Conservative Party in any election into a success, but the prime minister has managed it.

I blame the irresponsible broadsheet press. Since they had predicted a tremendous disaster, with the party holding only a handful of seats, the merely dreadful disaster it did suffer seemed like a victory by comparison.

There are two reasons why he will be less succesful at changing Prime Minister's Question Time. One is that there are too many people who think they can flatter, wheedle and cajole their way into government jobs, and some of them will be proved right.

Then there is TV. A five-second sound-bite is ideal for the news, but it will never furnish us with true enlightenment. In fact, the prime minister is often allowed to announce a change of policy – on Bosnia or some such – in relative peace. But the notion that his plan for topical questions, submitted the night before, will improve matters is obvious nonsense.

> *Mr Skinner:* 'I thank the Prime Minister for his courteous and helpful reply on the subject of the rail strike, and trust I shall not need to trespass upon his time and patience again.'

I don't think so.

15 June 1994

In mid-June Sir Norman Fowler announced that he would be stepping down as chairman of the Conservative Party.

It is always a sad day when Sir Norman Fowler resigns and frequency does not dull our regret. What I admire most about his appearances on the *Today* show (do they have any choice about which Tory they interview, or were they obliged by law to have Fowler?) is that he never made his explanations of each fresh electoral disaster sound merely routine.

He managed to inject a note of genuine synthetic anger when the interviewer suggested, for instance, that 18 out of 87 European seats might not be a frightfully good result. He always left the faint implication that criticizing the Conservative Party or government was the moral equivalent of insulting his mother.

No doubt his departure was one reason why Tory MPs seemed muted when Mr Major walked in. Their cheer was ragged, easily drowned by Labour's cheery blend of 'Resign!' and 'Don't Go!'

Mr Major's promise to change Prime Minister's Question Time has been fulfilled, at least in the sense that it is even worse than before. The French have the phrase: '*L'esprit de l'escalier*', meaning the brilliant retort you think of while going down the stairs on the way out of the *salon*.

These guys have *l'esprit* all right, only it's clutched tightly in their hands on their way up the stairs. Tossed a nifty feed line by, say, Madame de Staël: '*Tout comprendre rend très indulgent*, I always say. Don't you agree, Mr Major?' – he would fish out his bit of paper and say: 'I suppose there must be a time when you will address the current issue of the signalmen's strike,' as he did yesterday.

Margaret Beckett had arrived with her own witty repartee written out. She has been asking Mr Major to confirm the chancellor's statement that he is not going to reverse the coming tax rises. 'Two times in one week the prime minister has refused to answer. Let's try again. Taxes will go up next year, won't they? Just say yes.'

Mr Major said that she was 'wriggling and hiding behind promises [she] cannot substantiate'.

Mrs Beckett had another look at her piece of paper and found a reference to the chancellor's description of 'boom and bust economics'. 'Who do you think the chancellor was condemning: Lord Lawson as Mr Boom or yourself as Mr Bust?'

Mr Major replied, looking down at his file, 'Very well rehearsed, but it won't win you many votes.'

It was awful, like watching a double act who have never worked together before: Morecambe and Pace, perhaps, or Mike and Bernie Wise.

The prime minister was distinctly graceless towards Mr Paul Flynn, the one MP who had taken him at his word and sent him notice of the question he proposed to ask. Mr Flynn is shaping up as an effective one-man awkward squad, and the prime minister was right to be wary. But it bodes (as we say in Question Time) badly for the reforms if the first person to try them out is not only left unthanked but accused of 'scaremongering'.

17 June 1994

Debates on sex tend to be worthy and responsible, so I went over to the Lords yesterday with something to read – the official German-language guide to the Chamber. As I took my place overlooking the *Sitzungssaal*, the *Tagesordnung* were about to begin. The topic was the age of consent for homosexuals.

Lord McIntosh, for Labour, began with a calm sort of speech, saying that the Lords would be well advised to agree with the Commons and lower the age to 18. At one point he made a sly reference to Tory peers who had been to public schools, carrying the faint implication that the playing fields of Eton resembled the Dionysian bath houses of San Francisco.

Lords' *Sitzungsprotokolle* forbids barracking but the almost imperceptible rumblings, like thunder beyond a distant mountain range, were the equivalent of a full-scale shouting match in the Commons.

Next was Lord Simon of Glaisdale, once a Conservative minister, now a cross bencher. I was delighted to learn that 'cross benches' in German is *Querbanke*. (We are often told these days about the 'pink pound', a reference to the fact that many homosexuals are high earners who have no costly family responsibilities – and so, like Liberace, go crying all the way to the *Querbanke*.) I flipped to the French guide to check the Woolsack. It is, disappointingly, *Sac de Laine* and not 'pouffe'.

The Archbishop of York gave a first-rate impression of the Rev J C Flannel. The churches faced an 'agonizing issue'. He would not endorse the hatred and contempt felt for homosexuals. 'But we cannot say that homosexuals and heterosexuals are in all respects equivalent, because they are not.'

He concluded with a masterpiece of even-handedness: the age of 18, two years higher than for heterosexuals, was right because 'it says something about society's acceptance of heterosexuality as the norm'. By this time, the Archbishop was so firmly impaled on the fence, he was in danger of perforating himself along his own *Sitzungsplatz*.

Next we heard from the Earl of Arundel, the Earl of Surrey, Baron Beaumont, Baron Maltravers, Baron FitzAlan, Clun and Oswaldestre, and Baron Howard of Glossop.

This could have taken ages, but since they were all the same man, the Duke of Norfolk, and since he spoke for only 90 seconds, it was over very quickly. Homosexual acts were morally wrong and this was made clear in the Bible. Kinsey had claimed that ten per cent of men were homosexual, but the true figure in this country was 0.9 per cent. Homosexuality reduced life expectancy from 75 years to 42. Then he sat down.

Lord Skidelsky thought that a Roman Catholic like the duke ought to understand more about unfair discrimination – though it must be a long time since gangs of hooligans went out Duke of Norfolk-bashing.

Lord Longford rose. 'As my dear old friend A L Rowse said, the trouble with me is that I lack homosexual experience ... I wonder how many other noble lords lack homosexual experience? I do not see many hands going up ... I regard all human beings as equal in the sight of God, but I cannot say I am sorry that none of my children, my grandchildren, or my great-grandchildren, so far as I can see, are homosexuals. It is a great handicap in life ...'

Packenham burbled gently onward as we floated down to the sea, borne upon his stream of consciousness.

Then things got rather nastier. Lord Ashbourne said that homosexuality was 'unnatural and a perversion, and according to the Book of Leviticus, an abomination unto the Lord'. And sat down.

The trouble with quoting the Book of Leviticus, is that the old boy did cast his net rather wide. For example, the same text forbids us from eating lamb or beef fat, and recommends that we sacrifice turtle doves as a means of expiating our sins. Even Mr Howard, in his quest to go back to basics, has not yet recommended: 'Let 'em sacrifice a few turtle doves! That'll teach these youngsters what's what!'

In the end, some 71 peers went into the *Abstimmungswandelgang*, or division lobby, to vote for an age of consent of 16. But 245 voted against. (Later, after a speech by Earl Ferrers, who has said privately that he would like to see the gay age of consent raised to 94, but who supported the government view that 18 would have to do, the peers did vote to join the Commons and settle on 18.)

21 June 1994

A small moment of history: the term 'Lord Haw-Haw' was deemed unparliamentary language by the Speaker, and so joins a list of banned terms including 'ruffian', 'pharisee', 'cad', 'jackass' and 'pecksniffian cant'.

(Younger readers may need to know that Lord Haw-Haw was the nickname of William Joyce, an Irish-American who, like most members of the Irish World Cup football team, had an improbable British accent, hence his nickname. During the last war he broadcast talks from Germany designed to lower British civilian morale, but which had the contrary effect of cheering everyone up. In this respect he was the opposite of Tam Dalyell, the Labour MP against whom the phrase was originally used.

After the war Joyce was hanged for treason on the grounds that, having fraudulently obtained a British passport, he was nominally under the protection of the Crown – another example of creative British thinking which has made our relations with the Emerald Isle so difficult at times.)

I do feel that Mr Dalyell was being oversensitive. He had suggested that aerial photographs of fires in Iraq did not show villages being destroyed by Saddam Hussein's troops, but were traditional burning 'for hygiene reasons'.

This infuriated Emma Nicholson, the Conservative MP who has long campaigned for the Marsh Arabs. She called Mr Dalyell 'Lord Haw-Haw'. Mr Dalyell responded that this was not an acceptable term to describe 'those with whom one has a difference of opinion'.

I am a great admirer of Mr Dalyell's integrity and courage. But it did look as if he had – how can I put this? – decided to run the risk of appearing as an apologist for Saddam, and that goes some way beyond a 'difference of opinion'. I also suspect that the wretched inhabitants of Iraq would themselves have borne Mr Dalyell's hurt feelings with equanimity.

Later Harold Elletson introduced a bill to establish a national identity card scheme. This struck me as an excellent idea, since it might allow us to find out who Mr Elletson is.

I hadn't heard of him, and cannot recall ever seeing him. Nor do I know of him ever troubling the Hansard writers, though this may be ignorance on my part. In any event, he spoke enthusiastically about 'smart cards' which would encode everything about us, including our 'eye retina patterns'. I wondered whether he might not have wandered in one day in 1992, perhaps as a tourist, and been greeted warmly by policemen, staff and MPs who assumed he had been newly elected.

He would find the pleasant bars, the capacious toilets, and the reasonably priced restaurants. Now and again ministers would grasp him by the elbow, and ask for his support. At some point he decided to sit in the Chamber, and nobody stopped him.

Then he thought what a splendid idea a national identity card would be. Why not introduce a bill? By this time he was a familiar face; no one would be so rude to ask 'Are you a member?' so long after the election. Perhaps one day Mr Elletson will become prime minister, and what a wonderful tale that will be, fit for the pen of Jeffrey Archer!

23 June 1994

At the end of June, Mr Major attended the twice-yearly
summit meeting of EU heads of government, this time in
Corfu. There he used Britain's power of veto against Mr
Dehaene, the Belgian prime minister who was the choice
– willing or grudging – of the other eleven EU countries
to be president of the European Commission. Mr Major's
démarche magically restored his popularity in his own
party – even though Mr Dehaene was later replaced by
the prime minister of Luxembourg, a M Santer, who
turned out to share Mr Dehaene's views on all topics of
importance. However, this was not thought to matter.
The point was that Mr Major had taken a bold stand
against Franco-German hegemony.

It was as if we had woken up to hear Graham Taylor
announcing that not only had England played in the
World Cup finals, but had won. John 'Turnip' Major
arrived in the Chamber to roars of astonished applause
from the fans. Short of chanting 'They've all gone quiet
over there' and throwing a few bottles at the Serjeant at
Arms, Tory MPs could not have sounded more pleased.
Even fervent pro-European Tories congratulated him
(with the exception of Edward Heath, who now
constitutes a party of his own).

Labour tried hard to twist the knife, but couldn't even
get between his ribs. 'I made our strong views clear to the
Council,' he said. 'Very macho!' someone sneered, but
the jibe sounded wimpish in itself. 'The Corfu Council has
highlighted an issue of increasing concern ...' 'Your
incompetence!' they yelled, but for once very few Tories
were squirming.

The fact is – whatever the long term results turn out to
be – there are no votes to be lost being rude about a
corpulent Belgian with squinty eyes who thinks he knows
what's best for all of us.

(This national loathing of Belgians is new to me. Do
they beam out subliminal 'Hate Belgium' messages during

Neighbours? We don't even have a rude nickname for them yet, though it's urgently needed. How about 'fat, *frites*-eating Kraut-obeying *moules*-munchers'? It isn't snappy, but it covers the ground.)

Mr Major was as confident as I've ever seen him. 'Being a good European doesn't mean signing up to everything which our partners propose.' Who could disagree? Mrs Beckett for one. The weekend had been no triumph, but a humiliation for his tactics. Britain was now relegated to the European sidelines.

Tories started what they've rarely tried against a woman since She quit for Valhalla. (I have this vision of camp male Valkyries scooping her up into a chariot. Like Barbra Streisand, with her ridiculous voice and Big Hair, Lady Thatcher is in danger of becoming a gay icon.) Tories began an insidious crescendo murmuring, a wall of noise which rises and dips, and which can destroy a speech more effectively than heckling.

Mrs Beckett fought on, and accused the prime minister of being a prisoner of his own Euro-sceptics. He produced an anti-European quote from her chequerboard past, adding: 'I will spare you the other eight quotes which I have here ...' to Tory cries of 'More, more!'

It soon became clear that the man Major really wanted was Ruud Lubbers. Every time the Dutch premier was mentioned, he went into a moist-eyed encomium. One Labour back bencher asked politely just how the views of this paragon differed from those of the loathsome lowlander, Dehaene.

Mr Major began to recite a list of his qualities – a freetrader, a subsidiarist, an Atlanticist, a tan to die for (I made the last one up, but you get the general idea). He was so carried away one expected an invisible orchestra to strike up the first bars of 'Hello, Young Lubbers'.

Still no sign of the front-runner for the Labour leadership. To misquote Gertrude Stein, once again there was no Blair there. I am told he was in Monklands, campaigning for the Labour candidate in John Smith's old seat. But he'll have to turn up some time; he can't just descend from the skies next October.

28 June 1994

The Royal Family was much in the news towards the end of June. ITV devoted two and a half hours to a documentary about Prince Charles, which turned out to resemble an old-fashioned *Look at Life*, or a corporate video: 'Helping young people in today's world! Saving our environment! It's all in a day's work for Britain's future king!' The day before the programme was broadcast, Mr Tony Benn announced his own plans for the Prince.

We were in the stone entrails of Westminster Hall, the oldest public building in England, a few feet from where Sir Thomas More was tried. There, surrounded by photostats of ancient oaths and proclamations, and attended by TV crews, our modern courtiers, sat Tony Benn. He was overturning the constitution, again.

People accuse Mr Benn of being stark staring mad, and in many ways he obviously is. But the madness is prevented from soaring into the stratosphere by his sense of humour. For instance, he implied yesterday that his master plan – it is nothing less than to prevent Prince Charles from becoming king – might lead the Establishment to try to assassinate him. (Benn, that is, not Prince Charles.) One minute later a TV light fused, with a loud bang. 'Good God,' he said affably, 'they've shtarted already.

'Whenever you shuggesht a new idea,' he said with the

familiar sibilant 's', 'they shtart by shaying yurr mad, then they shay yurr dangeroush, then they shay yurr a fraud, and finally yer can't find anyone who didn't think of the idea firsht.'

And he'sh right. (Sorry, he's right; Mr Benn's tone of sweet amiability is quite infectious.)

This is how his plot will work. He has kept in his files ('for 59 years' – good grief, has he been planning this press conference since he was ten years old?) the proclamation which made Edward VIII king. This shows that the Privy Council, of which Mr Benn is a member, must agree to the new king 'with one Voice and Consent of Tongue and Heart'.

All he has to do, therefore, to stop Charles ascending the throne is to go to St James's Palace and make his objection known. It is in the taxi to the palace that he fears the assassination might take place. However, assuming his taxi driver can dodge the bombs, machine guns, howitzers and so on, Parliament will have to decide who gets the job, and Mr Benn will take the opportunity to propose an elected monarchy.

He was, he said in that tone of ingenuous good humour which makes his colleagues hate him so much, merely following the prime minister's example in Corfu, and insisting on the principle of unanimity.

He pointed out that the idea of an elected monarchy was not so unusual. The German emperor used to be chosen by, among others, the Electors of Hanover and Bavaria. Of course these electors were not your run of the mill serfs and peasants. They were magnificoes. 'When I went to Germany,' Mr Benn mused, 'I described myself as Elector of Chesterfield, and I was treated with a great deal of respect.'

He himself had taken the Privy Council oath, but under protest. 'At the end I said "but I don't agree with it". "You don't have to agree with it," they said, "we've

administered the oath." It was as if they had *injected* me
with it.'

Mr Benn began to lose me when be began a
complicated exegesis of the role of the Crown in our
constitution. What he missed was the fact that the
constitution has nothing to do with the case. The House
of Windsor has done what suits the House of Windsor for
decades now, whether it's paying tax, not paying tax,
shooting, abdicating or having affairs with married
women. As for ritual and ceremonial, they have people to
make it up, such as the Prince of Wales's weird
post-modern investiture.

By contrast, time-honoured Benn is an ancient part of
our nation's rich pageantry.

'Always good value, isn't he,' said an affectionate
cameraman as he packed up his gear. 'Never a dull
moment with Tone.'

29 June 1994

Day 49 since John Smith died, and still no Commons
sighting of Tony Blair (well, there's been one short
appearance, but apart from that we have seen neither
hide nor Blair).

Is he a victim of the signalmen's strike? Perhaps he's
reached London but wound up at the wrong station, like
Paddington Bear. Will a kind family find him in the left
luggage, a packet of marmalade sandwiches in his bag,
and a placard round his neck saying 'Please look after this
Blair'?

By contrast, Mrs Beckett is ubiquitous. The cover of
her colour campaign leaflet is a full-page picture of her at
a desk, looking statespersonlike. The effect is curiously

similar to the portrait of Lady Thatcher which used to hang in Conservative clubs all over Britain (and may still do so in some).

Inside Mrs Beckett is seen standing under what appears to be Britain's first space rocket, waiting to climb aboard for its maiden flight, to Blackpool. Near the back of the brochure she is standing with President Clinton, looking, it must be said, ill at ease.

Perhaps he had just invited her to come back to his motel. Or had omitted to do so. Either would create an embarrassing social situation.

But there is something suspicious about the picture. Maybe it is an illusion. Tourists in Washington like to be photographed standing beside life-size cardboard cut-outs of famous politicians. That could be the explanation. But where would the President have found a cardboard cut-out of Mrs Beckett?

An accompanying piece of paper invites readers to phone her campaign hotline, and to ask for 'Kevin or Ian'. It was this which amused the prime minister at Question Time. After an argument about the signalmen and the £800 a week pay rise just awarded to the chief executive of National Power (Mr Major takes the view that chief executives are beneficiaries of the magic of the market-place, which for some reason does not apply to more lowly workers, whose wages must be restricted by govern-ment edict), he said sarcastically: '... if members want to know more they should phone her campaign hotline, and ask for Kevin or Ian, who will explain her policies.'

At first I assumed that Kevin and Ian were Robert Maxwell's sons, anxious to turn an honest penny. Then it crossed my mind that they were refugees from *That's Life*, which has finally come to an end on BBC television. Mrs Beckett does look rather like Esther Rantzen. Kevin and Ian were clearly two of her ingratiating young men, or Esther's eunuchs as they were known in the BBC.

It's when Mrs Beckett suddenly switches from the scandal of low pay to wave a carrot with a willie at us that the transformation will be complete.

1 July 1994

> Through the year the Child Support Agency has been the subject of increasingly angry complaints from MPs. There has been a certain amount of embarrassment about this, since the House had passed the act setting up the CSA unanimously.

Everyone hammers on about Political Correctness, as if the greatest threat to our freedom were from people who said 'follically disadvantaged' instead of 'bald', not that anyone does, except in pubs where they make remarks like 'or circumferentially challenged, as I suppose we're meant to say now, hurr hurr'.

A greater threat is Political Incorrectness. If PC means making a political decision on the basis of an assertive dogma, then PI means taking a political decision and then inventing the dogma to rationalize it.

A classic example is VAT on domestic fuel. This had one purpose, to bring money into the Exchequer, but it was justified on the high-minded grounds that it would help prevent global warming. The public, being wise in the ways of politicians, and sceptical about the greenhouse effect and similar nonsense, rightly rejected this sophistry and the government lost a string of by-elections.

It was PI which also brought us the Child Support Agency. This was supposed to earn the chancellor around £300 million a year. But no minister could stand up and say 'We intend to reduce the borrowing requirement, cut taxes and so win the next election by squeezing absent fathers until they can pay no more or kill themselves, whichever comes first.'

So the CSA was presented as a great social reform, intended to create responsible fathers and permit single mothers to bring up well balanced, biddable children. There's also an element in the Labour Party which believes that all men are bastards, and the notion of the CSA appealed to them.

The effect was that Mr Donald Dewar, Labour's social security spokesman, found himself painted into a corner and had to restrain his attacks on, of all people, Peter Lilley, who has been Labour's demon king for quite some time. Mr Lilley had suggested in an interview that the criticism of the CSA came largely from journalists who had been caught by the agency. That's like saying that the attacks on Graham Taylor came from reporters who hadn't been picked for the England team.

Like PC, the curse of PI also breeds its own impenetrable jargon. There was plenty of that yesterday: 'parent of care', 'maintenance disregard', 'collusive desertion' and 'retrospective scoring' (something which would have helped England get into the World Cup).

I've nothing against jargon, since nobody could spell out in full what those phrases all meant every time they wanted to mention the idea. But I suspect that this breeze-block language tends to help construct bad, inflexible legislation, which may be one reason why we are in this pickle.

5 July 1994

Tony Blair finally came among us for a debate on the Police and Magistrates' Courts Bill. One felt like an inhabitant of Tanna, the South Pacific island where people believe the Duke of Edinburgh is a god. They may be victims of an irrational delusion, but they certainly look forward to his visits. So it is for us with Mr Blair.

(The Prince Philip cult was fostered in the 1970s by British officials who wanted Tanna to vote for our party rather than the French-backed one in the pre-independence elections. It was said that the duke would use his powers to bring prosperity to the island. These promises were extremely vague, but they did win the election – a familiar scenario.)

Yesterday's timing was crucial. The prime minister was not around, being in Scotland to greet the King of Norway. (It must be nice for Mr Major to meet royals who don't spend their leisure hours bed-hopping, but I do feel he should have been in Westminster facing MPs, not scraping to someone who is, after all, only a descendant of George V's little sister Maud.)

Anthony Steen introduced his bill to outlaw the use of the French language. I generally cringe when MPs try to be funny. However, this seemed to amuse them. The pleasure came less from the silly jokes about *negligées* making a *liaison dangereuse* somewhat *risqué*, but from the obsessive detail with which Mr Steen pursued his idea (designed, he said, purely to annoy French deputies who have passed a law to make English illegal in official documents).

How would he enforce the law? By having traffic wardens keep an ear cocked. Each use of a French word would bring a spot fine of £10. The whole farrago had the air of being cooked up by a lonely schoolboy in his bedroom.

Next, up sprang Mr Gyles Brandreth. (I recently appeared on a daytime television programme at the same time as him. I wondered how he might react to my criticisms of him in this column; even if he does not read the *Guardian*, the Commons is full of kind friends who would quickly point out any harsh words. In fact Mr Brandreth told me I had been 'effortlessly brilliant'. This was not sarcasm, as it would be with anyone else; he simply cannot help trying to insinuate himself with every single person he meets.) It must be rare for him to make an after-dinner speech for less than £3,000 – and so just at the moment MPs must have been reflecting on their good fortune at getting it free – in walked Mr Blair. Nobody noticed. It was a triumph.

His short speech, on involving local councils in crime prevention, was perfectly competent, emphasizing that it was 'this side which takes crime prevention seriously'.

He has a wide range of nervous hand gestures – palms spread out, banging the corner of the Despatch Box, or curled round like The Claw. (If Roy Jenkins appeared to be trying to cup the breasts of young peasant girls, Tony Blair looks as if he were trying to stop him.)

But the curious thing was the behaviour of the Tories. A whip, James Arbuthnot, walked up and down the government benches asking MPs to leave, presumably to deprive Mr Blair of an audience. Two Labour MPs spotted what was going on, and asked the Speaker to stop it. She airily replied that she was herself 'totally riveted' by the speech. Possibly, after so many months, she was trying to remember who this fresh-faced young man might be.

In any event, the Conservatives must be more afraid of Mr Blair than we knew.

(Mr Arbuthnot was also promoted in the reshuffle.)

6 July 1994

In July, the *Sunday Times* reported that two MPs had agreed to accept £1,000 each from a phoney businessman to table parliamentary questions. The revelation – the newspaper had dangled the bait in front of ten Labour and ten Conservative MPs, though only two Tories had nibbled – caused great outrage at Westminster. Naturally, as much of this was against the newspaper as against the MPs.

There was one topic of overwhelming interest to MPs yesterday, something which could hit them in all their wallets quite soon. It was the cost of funerals. Simon Hughes claimed that the cost of burying each stiff was about to rise from £50 to £150, a figure which would be 'appalling' for poorer parishioners.

Harry Greenway was outraged by 'conveyor belt cremations', at which the officiating minister might not even know the sex of the person being buried. (This is usually possible to work out from the name, unless the departed was called 'Leslie' or 'Pat' or 'Eddie Izzard'.)

In other words, there could be quite a nice little drink in it for a vicar who was prepared to put in a spot of overtime. And if he handled Four Funerals and a Wedding in one day, he might even be able to afford to table a parliamentary question.

Now the problem with this particular scandal was that Labour MPs had no real chance to sink their teeth into it. The Speaker told him she was looking into it urgently. In the meantime she would take no points of order.

Labour MPs grew increasingly desperate to find some way of raising the subject. Paul Flynn started by asking about tobacco companies which sponsor sport. 'It is damaging for our children that sponsorship of tobacco is displayed on the uniforms of sportsmen and women. Would it not be better for business sponsorship of MPs to be displayed on our suits, so the country could know who is filling the pockets of MPs?'

An excellent idea. The logos wouldn't be as snappy as Holsten or Camel, but they would command attention. For instance, Alistair Burt could have the British Fibreboard Packaging Association stitched on the back of his Cecil Gee. Others could have placards: 'Your Questions Answered. No Query Too Big or Too Small. 24-hour Service.' In these free market days, MPs could get the whole enterprise on to sound business lines. 'Yes, MR HOGRATH of BALACLAVA TERRACE! You have been selected by our computer for our Summer Special Offer: seven questions asked for only £5,000, a saving of Two Thousand Pounds! Imagine the envy of your neighbours in BALACLAVA TERRACE, MR SIMON HOGRATH, when they see you table your very own Parliamentary Questions – and we'll say a special "Thank You" with this gift of a handsome executive desktop pen set.'

Then came the points of order. (One wonders how much they cost. £250 for a real one, perhaps, rising to £5,000 for a bogus one.) 'On a point of order, Madam Speaker. Is it in order for the cafeteria not to serve Flora margarine, the scrumptious sandwich spread that's only slightly more dangerous than butter?'

Even Mr Graham Riddick, one of the two MPs involved, was prevented by an increasingly grumpy Speaker from demanding an inquiry into his own behaviour. I did some research of my own, and discovered that only four MPs have names which end in either 'nick' or 'dick'. How appropriate that half of them fell for the *Sunday Times* sting.

12 July 1994

If the prime minister decides to sack him, we will now have seen the last of Mr John Patten as education secretary. Some of us will be sorry.

Now I know that this column is often read in staffrooms – even as I write the smell of weak coffee and the fear of facing 5c again drifts back to me like the tea-soaked Hobnob – and I am well aware that Mr Patten is not popular in these places.

I've often wondered why. He is highly intelligent, and one of the wittiest MPs I know. His *pensées* on the social life of David Mellor when we passed a 'Private Shop' in Brighton were particularly amusing. He used to be a teacher himself.

Politically he was always thought of as a wet. That may be part of the problem. Many wets, when they saw that Mrs Thatcher was not some brief and terrible aberration, decided that to succeed they had to become just as Thatcherite as she was.

They adopted her dogmatic confidence. They concluded that, like all people who work for less money than their talent and diligence might command (other examples are nurses and BBC staff), teachers had to be punished for rejecting her free-market certainties. Worst of all, the wets confused her determination with pig-headed stubbornness. When Mrs Thatcher was about to lose a battle, she would generally change her mind before noisily proclaiming a triumphant success.

At the Charge of the Light Brigade, she would have taken one look at the Russian guns, wheeled about, and had the victory medals bestowed before anyone knew what was happening.

If this was to be his last hurrah, Mr Patten decided to go out with a final outrage. He pointed out that Harriet Harman, a member of the shadow cabinet, had decided to send her son to the Oratory, a grant-maintained school. This form of funding is strongly opposed by the Labour Party.

'It must make for very interesting discussions in the shadow cabinet where of course Mrs Taylor [the education spokesperson] sits in firm favour of abolishing such schools altogether,' Mr Patten said.

Tony Blair has been considering whether to send a child to the same school. Luckily it is a Roman Catholic establishment, because some Jesuitical reasoning is required here. According to Labour Party teachings, it is all right to send your child to a grant-maintained school, since you have virtually no direct choice in the way it is funded. This is quite different from sending him or her to a public school, because there you have to make your own, personal decision to cough up the money. So there you are. Say three Hail Marys and recite Clause IV.

The whole row (the prime minister also referred obliquely to Mr Blair's possible choice, but then Mr Blair is the original of the man who wasn't there in the old doggerel. 'He wasn't there again today / Oh how I wish he'd go away') infuriated Mr Derek Enright, who complained to the Speaker.

'I don't think that Members' children from any side should be used in politics,' said Betty, robustly. I think she is wrong. The decision about where a child goes to school is generally made by its parents. If the parents are politicians, and appear to hold the view that what's good enough for other people's children isn't good enough for their own, that's a perfectly legitimate subject for discussion.

Back to Mr Patten, who I shall miss if he goes. I see him, with his extravagantly stagey gestures, his independently waving hair, his nimble footwork which only we, sitting above him, can admire, as less of a politician than an actor-manager in the old tradition – perhaps like J Barrington Minge, a character created by Peter Sellers.

Sellers had a routine in which the astrakhan-collared

Minge goes from shop to shop, demanding the finest goods, trying to pay with an increasingly bedraggled cheque. In the end even the Chinese laundry turns him down.

'Well, would you mind ironing the bloody thing?' he asks with grandiose bravura. Minge would have been proud of John Patten.

13 July 1994

The affair of the £1,000 questions dragged on. The Speaker had ruled that she would 'give precedence' to a motion sending the affair up to the privileges committee, which is actually an ad hoc collection of grandees mustered for the process. This motion traditionally goes through on the nod but this time there was a full-scale debate first.

Conservatives were united in their rage against the men who had brought shame upon their party and the stench of bribery to the parliamentary process.

They seemed to have few complaints about the MPs who had agreed to take the money for asking questions. But they were furious with the *Sunday Times* for exposing them. By contrast, Labour MPs were delighted. 'The *Sunday Times* should be congratulated!' said David Winnick. Clare Short announced that 'The *Sunday Times* has done British democracy a favour.' If Rupert Murdoch had walked in, they wouldn't have known whether to spit at him or hug him.

But the Tories were very cross. David Ashby (C A & P Tools and Products, GPM (Displays) Foam Board Manufacturers – I quote from the Register of Members'

Interests) wanted a thorough inquiry into the *Sunday Times*.

Roger Gale (Scottish & Newcastle Breweries, Rhone Poulenc Rorer Ltd, Organon UK Ltd) angrily demanded to know why the paper had felt it necessary to resort to subterfuge.

Patrick Nicholls (Hill & Smith Holdings, Federation of Associations of Specialists and Sub-contractors, Port Enterprises Ltd, Howard de Walden Estates, Minotels Europe Group, and on to the crack of doom) demanded that the paper be forced to declare who their original informant had been.

John Gorst, of John Gorst & Associates, a 'business and public affairs consultancy', then made a speech of majestic pomposity. He described at length how the *Sunday Times* had tried to set him up (one wondered what could have made the paper think that the blameless Mr Gorst might ask money for carrying out parliamentary duties?). A young man had asked him to table the question, and had then proposed the bribe.

'I explained to him that it was not proper for an MP to accept money for tabling questions. While it might not be illegal, it was not very nice.'

'Not very nice!' scoffed Labour MPs, smug in the knowledge that none of their lot had accepted the bung.

Dale Campbell-Savours (Lab nothing lucrative really) asked what the difference was between taking money for a one-off service and taking even larger sums for a permanent 'consultancy'.

Mr Gorst did not answer, but moved on to what was meant to be a thunderous peroration against the press. 'Never has there been such contemptuous arrogance since the days of the robber barons.'

He said that he had clearly been bugged in the precincts of the House itself. 'There is no specific reference to bugging in Erskine May ...' he remarked, not surprisingly, since the sage of parliamentary practice was writing in the 1840s, when if you wanted to bug someone, you had to hide a stenographer in your baggiest plus-fours.

Tony Benn saw Gorst off. In a speech which began ambitiously by denouncing Magna Carta itself (the way he put it, it sounded like a Cones Charter for rich landowners) he declared: 'We are public servants. I would not dream of asking for money either as an individual, or by setting myself up as a consultancy. We are elected to be consultants to the British people.'

Graham Riddick, one of the two paid inquisitors, rose. He apologized. He grovelled. He wheedled and whinged. He had been guilty only of a lack of judgement, he said. He had been 'unwise'. But he was the victim of a 'scam'. Heep-like, he whined that he had brought embarrassment to the prime minister at the time he was 'abroad, fighting for Britain's interests'.

It was ghastly. I reeled out, feeling sorriest for the wretched civil servants who have to answer these questions. If MPs can get £1,000 for asking them, shouldn't they get at least twice that for digging out the replies?

14 July 1994

With Parliament about to rise for the summer, we had the last Prime Minister's Question Time without Tony Blair. Assuming that he wins the Labour leadership election, even he may feel obliged to turn up at the Commons on 18 October.

He doesn't have to. It's only a convention, invented by Harold Macmillan, that the prime minister answers questions twice a week. Mr Blair might prefer to spend his time in TV studios. I am not being facetious. Many politicians greatly prefer TV studios to the floor of the House, and not only because of the free gin and solicitous make-up ladies.

Television still has an old-fashioned respect for the democratic process. It allows politicians to talk uninterrupted and, unlike the Commons, does not expect complicated arguments to be reduced to snappy sound-bites.

MPs tend to be trivial entertainers, like Gyles Brandreth, whereas television still attracts serious persons who concern themselves with the issues, such as Jeremy Paxman, and the great dynasty of Dimblebys. (Did you know that there is a third brother, a sort of Gummo Dimbleby, Nick, who so far as we know has never been on television?)

I do not sense that Mr Blair will be elected on a huge tide of affection. For years the Labour Party has defined itself by its internal enmities. Its members are rather like the people of Lilliput, racked by a dispute over which end of an egg you should crack open first. John Prescott is a big-ender, Margaret Beckett switched from little to big and back again. Blair thinks the whole silly row is a waste of time, and no attitude could be more infuriating to the true partisans.

Mrs Beckett has done well against Mr Major. Her questions have been short and crisp, and have sometimes unsettled him. Yesterday, for instance, she wanted to know about a leaked letter Kenneth Clarke had sent to a constituent. In this he had said that too many things were exempt from VAT. The prime minister was reduced to blustering that extending the tax to fares, books and children's clothes was 'NOT ... POLICY ... NOW!', which came over as less ringing than he had perhaps hoped.

Mr Simon Burns asked a greasy question about the new

OECD report which evidently depicts Britain as an economic Elysium where plump, wingèd cherubs fly over gambolling workers and their contented families.

What an idiot! Mr Major has decided all his ministerial changes by now, so Mr Burns was wasting his breath.

20 July 1994

This prediction proved completely wrong. The following day Mr Major gave young Burns his first ministerial job. Of course he might have made this decision weeks before. On the other hand, he could have said to himself at this precise moment, 'Heavens, what a greasy fellow, a positive KY jelly baby among MPs! I shall certainly reward him with a job!'

It was the first bloodless reshuffle. Sacked ministers avoided the humiliation of being summoned to Number Ten and walking out – in front of the TV cameras – to find their official cars had already gone to pick up their successors. John Major had dismissed them, ever so discreetly, the previous night.

Why is Mr Major especially annoying when he's being most kind and thoughtful? Doesn't he realize that the public expects and needs blood? The ritual abasement of people who once held power over us is essential to democracy. Here's the man who once decreed what our children should learn, and where is he now? Waiting for a bus in Whitehall, ha, ha!

Nothing against the individuals concerned. Being sacked is as wounding for a minister as it is for anyone else. You might think they would see it as part of the hurly-burly, the knockabout of politics, but they don't. I know a minister who will still tell you at great and bitter length how Mrs Thatcher fired him – 13 years ago. When Norman St John Stevas was kicked out of the cabinet, a colleague and I thought to send him a jokey cartoon card with the message: 'Sorry to hear you're leaving.' He hasn't spoken to me since.

But ministers are not Mr Perkins being made redundant after a lifetime's service in the sales department. They are our rulers, and suffer they must.

So yesterday's scenes in Downing Street were deeply smug. Only winners were on parade. At 9 o'clock Mrs Shephard arrived, looking smug. Five minutes later Mr Jeremy Hanley turned up, looking equally pleased with himself.

It's a well known fact, repeated on TV yesterday that the new Tory chairman's father was Tommy Handley, the radio comedian who kept Britain laughing during the blitz. He had a pair of comical pants, which said 'I belong to Tommy Handley' as he walked along. One could almost hear his son's newly promoted trousers murmuring proudly: 'I belong to the chairman of the Conservative Party.'

Sadly, like so many well known facts, it isn't true. Mr Hanley's father was Jimmy Hanley, an actor. Towards the end of his career, Mr Hanley Sr took part in a programme on ITV called *Jim's Inn*, which pretended to be a normal chat show, but was in fact a string of hidden commercials, thus making an even better metaphor for the present Conservative Party.

Mr David Hunt came and left looking thoughtful. His new job as civil service minister means that he has the job of keeping other ministers up to scratch. We are officially briefed that he will be known as 'The Enforcer' – and a less likely Arnold Schwarzenegger it would be hard to imagine. If he were to say to the new employment secretary: '*Hasta la vista*, baby,' Mr Portillo would think it no more than a courteous farewell.

Viscount Cranbourne was the most surprising new cabinet minister, bringing the House of Cecil back into government. This was less surprising if you knew that he was a member of the Blue Chips, a sort of super-Freemasons within the party.

Blue Chips were once vaguely left-wing Tories elected in 1979. They eat dinners at Tristan Garel-Jones's house. I won't say they're smug too, but they do eat off table mats decorated with a collective portrait of themselves.

John Major is a member, and so is John Patten. Patten had to be replaced, otherwise only three members of the cabinet – the others are William Waldegrave and Ian Lang – would know the secret handshake (or now, the rolled-up talking trousers).

Jonathan Aitken looked sombre, surprisingly, since he has now made it to the cabinet after nearly 21 years in Parliament. In the 1970s he and Carol Thatcher had a long relationship which ended in tears; her mother refused to talk to him, let alone promote him. Marrying the boss's daughter is one thing; giving her the push is quite another.

Over on College Green, the survivor of another unwise liaison, David Mellor, was talking about the need to 'get the right bottoms on the right seats', advice he should have heeded himself.

In the House, Michael Heseltine – the real victor of the reshuffle, since he told the prime minister where he would not go, and he wenteth not – was answering questions. Back benchers rose to heap praise upon the government. Hartley Booth, the unthinking man's David Mellor, praised its industrial policy. David Amess denounced the 'politics of envy'. It seemed a bit late, like buying a crate of Scotch the day after the Budget.

But sycophancy in the service of ambition is, like painting the Forth Bridge, a job that never ends.

21 July 1994

Tony Blair was elected Labour leader the following day.

It fell to the party's chairman, David Blunkett, to introduce Mr Blair as its new leader, and for a moment we feared it might be a case of the blind leading the bland. But the speech was much better than that; it was tough, angry, but also optimistic. It spoke to the party's heart as well as its head. This, one felt, was a speech which would not only bring in the voters, but also bring out the party's workers.

(I am often puzzled why people assume that Mr Blair became favourite for the job simply because he was 'good on television'. I don't think he is especially good on television. He blathers sometimes, and appears evasive. What he is good at is that older political skill, oratory.)

Not that many workers of any kind were around for yesterday's coronation. Glossy suits, silk ties, expensive haircuts – and that was just the trade union leaders, who were banished to the back of the hall behind the TV cameras, quite literally to the outer darkness. No one wanted the day to be spoiled by an unexpected glimpse of Jimmy Knapp.

It was a day out for the new Labour aristocracy: successful lawyers such as Helena Kennedy and Geoffrey Bindman, women in suits lugging vast soft leather briefcases which you knew contained three think tank reports, a week's shopping and a couple of nappies. There were chaps in pony tails, and several very rich men such as David Puttnam and Clive Hollick.

Held in a small basement, the meeting had something of the air of a trendy night club. One suspected there were frightfully civilized bouncers on the door to keep the ugly people out.

The chatter was of the Dordogne, and when the delegates were going to arrive for their holidays. Invitations to take part in the annual Labour Party *v.* the

Guardian cricket match there were tossed around. I was glad to be going somewhere else. Who would want to take the risk of catching Harriet Harman out?

John Prescott may have been the only horny-handed son of toil there, and even he ended the meeting blowing out luvvie kisses into the hall.

I don't want to be alarmist, but the middle classes are back in charge of Labour (some might argue that they never lost control; it's just that they choose to dress middle class now). They will celebrate Mr Blair's victory with glasses of Montbazillac while listening to *The Archers* or fitting new doors to their French farmhouses – louvres for Labour.

The lights went down for the results. The winner was – Tony Blair! The lights stayed down for a while, encouraging us to believe that the new modern Labour Party wasn't quite as efficient as we'd been told. As Mr Blair began speaking, the giant white rose behind him was touched by a spotlight with the faintest blush of pink. The shade grew sharper and more scarlet, until at the end the whole stage was bathed in the rose's hue.

The speech worked because he presents Labour as a national party facing a national crisis, not merely a collection of factions. 'I shall not rest until once again, the destinies of our people and our party are joined together in victory.'

The most effective part of the speech came early on, when he used what is clearly going to be a standard rhetorical device, the rolling sentence. This continues, clause after clause, mounting up to, in one case 56 words, in another 61, as if the monstrosities of Conservative rule are too great to leave time for breathing or punctuation.

Towards the end he talked about a revolution, but one which could not come overnight – it would arrive through hard work, courage and persistence, as had happened in South Africa.

By chance, my next appointment was at Lords, for the first cricket Test between England and South Africa for 29 years. I sat amid a group of white South Africans who were cheering the white South African team while waving the brand new black South African flag.

The privileged waving the banner of the dispossessed, while drinking rather a good cold Chardonnay – there's a symbol for the new Labour Party!

(This was also the Test in which England's young, fresh-faced new skipper was caught rubbing dirt into the ball. But that's quite enough political metaphors for one year.)

22 July 1994